WALKING

Walking

A collection of poems
by

PATRICK HURLEY

BOOKS

Adelaide Books
New York / Lisbon
2020

WALKING

A collection of poems

By Patrick Hurley

Published by Adelaide Books, New York / Lisbon
adelaidebooks.org

Editor-in-Chief
Stevan V. Nikolic

For any information, please address Adelaide Books
at info@adelaidebooks.org

or write to:

Adelaide Books
244 Fifth Ave. Suite D27
New York, NY, 10001

ISBN: 978-1-949180-73-2

Printed in the United States of America

To Teresa

"Walker, there is no road, the road is made by walking."

– Antonio Machado "Proverbs and Songs"

01.01

from the steppes come
deep breathing
and an oriental chord
progression
is this some waking dream?
nightmare more like …
pervasive smell of old
man aftershave
whose slightly spicy
note cannot
cancel the must of death

lack of trees and
temperature extremes
foster what might be called
flattening of affect

what hebephrenic
verse forms could
possibly withstand
the wind's
relentless onslaught?

questions arise about
for example
average annual rainfall
to a cow or other ruminant
is there really any difference
between the steppe
and the pampas?

where to go from here
is always the question
but like all questions
worth asking
it has no answer

the only solution
if you could call it that
is the automatic revival

01.02

what diluted
truth breaks upon
the poisoned shores
of memory?

a strained voice
attempts to cry out
but as in this dream
and every other
only strangled
inarticulate
moans escape

01.03

apocalyptic lighthouse
with minor chord progressions
that's what it is
dyspeptic cellos
file for unemployment

rotting flower petals
rise up from the concrete
i recognize the phenomenon
subtle reaction to
offensive tempos

what mortal foot or ear
i ask you
could dance to
this asymmetry?

01.04

ashtabula i hear—
i know instinctively
it's a place name
so without hesitation
i set off on foot

a fine rain falls
i've walked this road
perhaps many times

blue-green cypress
fronds enclose me
they seem weighted
with the dew of truth

there must once have been
many seekers on this path
but their skinny legs
ceased to support them

they sought eternal light
but ended up a few
minor constellations
in the celestial firmament

01.05

a rapid high-pitched summons
directs me to no
known latitude
navigation was never
my strong suit

somehow i find myself in the
shadow of the broken
bell tower
both pitch and tempo
are brought
low by agencies unseen

watery labyrinths threaten
to achieve their fell purpose
until a polish count traps them
in time's crystalline structure

01.06

gregorian warnings
no one can make out
perhaps because
they are uttered in
some previously
unknown slavic tongue

they whisper
sounding now
somehow more insistent
at this terminally
reduced volume

01.07

observations exert
dynamic opposing forces

silver bells peel
as a strong wind
cuts through the woods

someone is preparing
a seasonal apparatus
but already
the sky grows dark
begging the question

the question?

01.08

a drumming a thumping
urgent progression
into abysses
only then the
deliberation sublime

hollow methods
shape the void
into geometric
substance

elusive meaning
but efficient
exegetical machinery

nonetheless
the hammer keeps falling on
nothing

01.09

desperate minds
fix themselves
upon the trill

melancholy minds
will find
no succor here

somber tones
turn out to be
relentless

if a bird flies
into a window
will not his
song be altered?

utilitarian messages
will take on the
fragile sheen of
psychotic beauty

01.10

perilous sawing
across channels
some seek the
rice paddies of infinity

true desperation
is international
scarcely is it assuaged
by mere rising tempos

sopranos shout 'timber!'
so those below
might be prepared
if you hear the crash
it didn't kill you

01.11

slender couplings
sound like the
horn of romance
but the poison mushroom
never sits well

before long aloof voices
will chant their vague
empty promises and
you will feel as if
you have gorged
on too many sweets

what then?

a fine white powder
is in itself
neither good nor bad
but the spores of
disaffection are legion

the hose of uneasiness
never gets kinked
and the weeds it
constantly waters
will develop a
most handsome
violet tinge along
the edges of their leaves

01.12

some would pull
the myriad strands
together into
a skein of half-meaning
ask yourself
is it ever worth it?

indifferent cypresses
encircle the abandoned mine
the density of patience
renders the air
un-breathable
waiting is
only ever waiting
never for

the surface of joy
is deeply scarred
but boredom's patina
suggests sustained use

even ruins pass away though
dead matter in no way implies
a teleological imperative

the densely patterned carpet
of meaning will unravel
one thread at a time
and much of
what was taken
for the units of beauty
was just metaphysical dirt
ground into the
screaming fibers
of the quotidian by an
infinity of ill-fitting boots

01.13

bellicose tones
introduce
an uncertain theme

electric hum
perceptible beneath
the skin of
nature's imposture

an equivocal
hymn of praise
is drowned out
by the organ's
rich drone

absolute silence
seeks return

01.14

light refracts through
mute runes of ice
these are mental formations

the late heat of the year
disallows such feeble
attempts at communication

a fine strand
must float just beyond
the apprehension of the senses

and what if this strand
were to vibrate
at just the right frequency?

could this information
reach us
or possibly be decoded?

01.15

planetary death throes
with bleeps and squeaks
duration is a necessary fiction

terrifyingly dulcet tones
are in the end a cul de sac

now (if we can use a word
so demonstrably void of sense)
erosion works its subtle magic

metallic cicadas buzz on
beyond any realistic
life expectancy
and idle talk of
thermodynamics is silenced

who would have thought
that the insistent
beat of misery
would be so danceable?

01.16

extension is hectic and
its dense traffic
is nerve wracking

to perceive
the cycle and
effortlessly enjoy
eccentric orbit
offers at least
a slender chance
of transcendence

grim fears of repetition
are offset by
heraclitian rearguard tactics

subtle utterances
are hard to decode
until ubiquitous
noise is filtered
there is an
auditory window
and whispers
can be seen

travel in dreams
and let stillness be
a new form of mobility

01.17

the mystical significance
of certain secret numbers
proves a poor starting point

patterns both natural
and unnatural
deflate the potential
of non-linear methodologies

all radical departures
signal the arrival of
orthodoxies
even if slightly delayed

inversion of absolutes
was never an adequate
escape plan

there are strange energies
crackling in the atmosphere
just beyond the limits
of rational thought
these highly charged particles
cannot be categorized
once they reveal themselves
their attraction is
irresistible and irrevocable

do not ask after madness

01.18

stunted trees line the edges
of this epistemological route
a sudden realization—
not one has ever had leaves

and you—for all your
knowledge of solid
geometry—
what will you do
when confronted with these
never-before-seen shapes?

what limited color palette
could describe a sudden freeze?

categorical confinement
has rendered us immune to
the chromatic intensity of
unknown forms

01.19

on the axis
voices balance
precariously

in the distance
an echo that sounds
like 'absalom'

hot and cold will exist
in perfect equipoise on
the day confusion's
vast mural is
finally painted over
with a thick gesso of
brilliant white

01.20

dark visions in
northern climes

echo's palsy hesitates
on the brink
but most are trapped
in briar tangles

there is but one chance
to cross the arid
plains of reason
most never make it alive

stochastic warbling
forms a tightly woven
sonic barrier but
intrepid drunkards
break through
and are transformed

the quality of the light
and the fine gradations
of ambient temperature
are finally discernible

01.21

and the thirty
longshoremen of perfection
will whisper into your ear
the great secret

each of these sounds
will seem frightening
and alien at first but
taken together the aggregate
will suggest a map
leading to higher places

only fear and indecision
will bar the pilgrim from
the true pattern
imprinted upon death's
cartographic structure

listen to the voices that
will lead you to the water

be careful not to drown

01.22

ephemeral tape loops and
squeaks winding down

the phantom taste of tart apple
gives warning against
the fierce dogs of stupefaction

rancid grease particles
hang heavy in the air

plotlessness describes
the aimless wanderings
within the confines
of perception

the crickets will set sail
in cylindrical boats
as the sea takes on
a reddish cast

blow the shofar of boredom
if you dare

01.23

no one is prepared to dance
the intellect is a rusted cage

to those with dull senses
music is noise and
noise is music

all sensation is muted by
rote expectation

can calloused feet
ever come into contact
with the parquet of
exquisite gyrations?

glossy black ink marks
signify nothing
your language elevates
the inarticulate grunts
of beasts to
the gospels of mediocrity

hear in my ululations
the song of the real

01.24

the ink of lucidity
undercuts itself by
never fully drying
the wisdom it limns
only ever appears
as a smudge

skillful hands
rapidly produce
the calligraphy of
deception

to write this down
now is to lie
how to go beyond
these words?

01.25

and now sound ceases

the interminable
repeating pattern
is displaced by
an unfolding blackness
of silence whose
structure and texture
are just as complex
as what came before

contrary to expectations
the other senses are dulled
rather than sharpened

nostalgia for those
faded notes is keen
like the sensation
of a phantom limb

i kiss the missing
hand of blaise cendrars
and gradually hear
two minor chords alternate

01.26

sudden drops in altitude
rupture solitude
here/hear
the vibrant colors fade

a single strand
of viscera vibrates
and high frequency
waves subdue us
with their incessant
tones of subtle disquiet

01.27

museums house
time's detritus

the four naked
curators
will slouch
through the mud
towards some
rusted bethlehem

no star will
guide them and
a surfeit of
physical flesh will
not make up for
a lack of wisdom

02.01

this is the tabula rasa
another dubious opportunity
monumentally squandered

what is excessive qualification?
or the science of the so-called?

a somber aura cannot protect
against shifting tempos

this sense of urgency
cannot be measured

mystic transubstantiations
will change dead matter
into pure energy

02.02

the mystical preoccupations
of lean finns
transpire equivocally

rising tones and major
chords form recognizable
melodies of deception

await the martial blasts that
signal eclipses of discordance
and the sharp tang
of disaffection

02.03

miniature forces exact
disproportionate results

a forgotten people use
mysterious practices against
the fabrics of high
tensile strength

in the heart of the forest
laughable modernities perish

confused multitudes will never
decipher the original script

immersion in dark sonorities
is talismanic but
protection itself is no guerdon

02.04

there is no port of entry
what atlas charts these
saturnine territories?

ingress is a dangerous fiction
radioactive particles
are ubiquitous

toxic energies fix our hopes
but only choice computes

02.05

these voices are not french
and this is no paradise

try for a somber tone but
mandatory laugh tracks
will make mock

uneasiness like incessant
drumming on the hollow
reeds of deconstruction

experience shears off
limbs at oblique angles

there is something in the east
but its name is
unpronounceable

02.06

gross appetites
do not always mislead
learn each name
only to forget it

sounds strike from odd angles
reminding the
incredulous that
life might be after all one
long allergic reaction

02.07

dark coincidence
under overcast skies
metaphysics and meteorology
will collide

utter meaningless
enjoys unspeakable density

02.08

malevolent gestures
dissipate as
reason lurches towards
its final resting place

the once nourishing loaves of
conventional wisdom are
ergot-laden slices of
spasmodic madness

voices raised in prayer
spark now in the
animal heart only terror

02.09

within the sphere
reside certain clues
but a toxic miasma
surrounds and
protects this circular
illumination

it must be approached
from the tangent
too much care however
in calculating
arcs and apothems
spells disaster

searching for the
formula is pointless
equations shift even
as we write them
and the standard
symbols dissolve into
ciphers that no longer signify

02.10

a metal wire stretched taut
is not a metaphor
let alone a metonymic
construct

if a hammer should
strike it a note will sound
the senses are said
to be allied to reality

all sensory data
are ephemeral and
a lifetime's accumulation
of such dubious evidence
amounts to a finite number
of microscopic particles
on a frictionless surface

02.11

a grammatical
structure cannot
explain time's progression

all is disposition
and rearrangement
heed the monitory chord

the big truths sought for by
mediocrity's inner circle
are hidden in the shadows
cast by subatomic particles

02.12

this duality or
any other misleads
they are dangerous constructs

hollow institutions
foster misleading techniques

the path is already
beneath the hiker's feet
to seek it is to go astray

the sound of a flute and
the pungent flavor of garlic
cannot be separated

stop listening to the voices
and you will hear them

02.13

no breeze relieves
the stagnant air
sporadic mushrooms
dot the landscape

there is a gate
beyond which stands
a baroque tower
invisible to the naked eye

confused schematics in blue
attempt to explain
the mechanisms of obfuscation

the light will take on
a strange intensity
and the foliage
will grow
intensely aromatic

omnipresent energy
hums and crackles
does the faint horn blast
in the distance signal
victory or impending doom?

02.14

decapitated flower blossoms
carpet the sterile ground
frenetic strings send up
a wail of despair

a sense of anxiety
will expand beyond
all reasonable parameters
and the time will seem ripe
for eschatological
interpretations

02.15

all the vowels have dropped
out of the deceptively easy
to pronounce bromides
of reason
leaving behind harsh
guttural grunts of indignation

and now mutually exclusive
tones sound simultaneously
what profound discord
will follow?

02.16

the bed is burning
but the sleepers sing on
unaware of
the inexorable peril

a draining away
of essence is at work

some will adopt
a posture of prayer
and some will lament
what they call erroneously
the passage of time

both time and prayer
are consumed in
the blue flames

what body of water will
reflect the ghost of matter?

02.17

gradually the strings
come together
forming a tight web
vertigo descends
all is confusion

structure will dry up
the desiccated turnip
of spatial order will
wither completely

flatulent geometers
reel helplessly around
some non-euclidean space
clutching their
distended bellies

three primary colors
will merge
and from what once
was thought sterile
one slender shoot
will emerge

02.18

eccentric symbols
scrawled hurriedly—
some slender alien
evidence will be left behind

there is a plotless story
that need not be told

follow the spiraling digressions
resistance is expected and
factored into the flow's
nefarious pattern

doing nothing at all
is the radical gesture
against which
there is no defense

02.19

sounds announcing royalty
degenerate into
sonic flatulence
diminished expectations and
a metaphysical toothache
set the stage for
what is to come

men continue to blow
their horns but
the hibiscus is already
withering

ascend the mountain path
the air is thin but
so are the crowds

neither the destination
nor the pace is important
just keep moving

when the dirge sounds
back in the distance
just keep laughing

02.20

there is no passage
not of time
nor through space
we cover what
should be uncovered
unearth what belongs
beneath the surface

dubious structures
erected at night—
neither scale them
nor work your way
painstakingly
around them

pass through them
as if they are not there

they are not

02.21

memory is fragmentary
there is nothing to be
assembled or reassembled

beware the cyclical
fallacy as well as
totality's siren song

can a solitary particle
admit of possession
even while aggregates
shift and morph
relentlessly into
brightly colored patterns?

seductive … but in the end—
if there is such a thing—
merely hypnotic or
narcotic
perhaps even
arteriosclerotic

02.22

escape as a concept
is pure distraction

effective movement
towards any cardinal point
must be predicated upon some
subtle interior transformation

even from the standpoint
of a supposed
objective observer
situated let's say in such a way
as to observe without
influencing the observation

even such an observer
could track no movement
that wasn't insincere

the language of exteriority and
directionlessness will
forever mark
our circumambulations

02.23

the gates seem forbidding
but stout souls will enter
at first the music from
within will sound dark
if not discordant

change your ears

simplicity contains within it
the root of all complexity

abandon serial fantasies
repetition doesn't exist

there is a sound
imperceptible to dull ears
the crowds will laugh and jeer
when you start to dance

pity those who will
never hear the music

02.24

nature is not a uniform
shade of green and
old walt never measured
the handkerchief of the lord

abide with me in
contradiction

i'll grow so vast
all opposites will
be contained within me
nations and churches
will cease to exist

everything decays in time
what rich black
compost it all makes

02.25

the beggars from porlock
will try to derail your thoughts
'excuse me!' they'll shout
over and over again
just when you thought
you might be on to something

they're looking for
metaphysical spare change

don't try to get back on track
that train has gone—
ferrying the dead-eyed hordes
across rivers

acheron
cocytus
lethe
phlegethon
styx

back to their suburbs

02.26

the powers that sustain
are the powers that destroy

for the moment
i hold them
in perfect equipoise

02.27

the ubiquity of
a certain number
must limit neither
our vision nor our
mathematical
imagination

for some three and
four are touching
to others separated
by an infinity of points

they are both wrong
and both right

there is a subtle harmony
don't let the bars
of its staff imprison you
concentrate on the spaces
between the lines

03.01

though the
simultaneous
mesh of time
suggests a new
understanding of
determinism

what precarious life
can do without
boethian synthesis?

03.02

passage through
monitory straits
without incident
this the verbless
miracle where
inaction posits action

slinking and skulking
must be rejected
the bold strut
requires no guides or maps

not deciding is
not the same as indecision
our movement is frictionless

others are mired in patterns
and textures they no longer see
though they've spent this life
and all the others
weaving them

unravel

03.03

the silence of tradition
casts no shadow
the shifting moment
approximates eternity

an infinitude of voices
cry out in a wilderness
of their own making

are planetary disturbances
at the root of all malaise?
life itself is just
retrograde motion

03.04

the sap-filled crevice
exudes the life force
all life is green

those who cannot
see smell taste
are dead tissue animated
by a malignant energy

03.05

if a sound suggests
enclosure
stop your ears

expansion and contraction
coexist in a single moment
confinement to a single space
requires special concentration

when the fixed patterns
begin to shift
raised voices will be lowered

the music grows
more beautiful
as it approaches silence

03.06

reality itself is distortion
there is something
outside and beyond
or inside deep within

there are radical variations
and subtle deviations

there must be a way beyond

literal paths and metaphorical
ones amount to the
same thing

vision begins with the
refinement of perception

03.07

mysterious rites and
rituals are irrelevant

the right hand path
is touted loudly
though virgil led
dante to the left
all but twice

catalog all you can
say you know truly know
then jettison it

such knowledge
though weighing little
is surprisingly cumbersome

03.08

flailing and wallowing
in sublunary imperfection—
internal ascension
to other realms
requires no ladder

the retreat from
the city of man is a
casting off or a casting away
in every sense

tiny divinities float in
the ambient air
invisible to the untrained eye
easily popped by the
grubby hands of
malevolent children

some will float beyond
their grasp
and high-pitched
lamentations will
fill the lower realms while

the unmoored ones
float peacefully away

03.09

primary colors
disassociate themselves
from the muddled aggregate

five repeated notes
gradually give way to
sun-drenched west-african
polyrhythms

the great dance begins—
all the sinews will be
visible beneath the skin
once the fat is cut away

03.10

what inheres or coheres?
what is assemblage?
if we find the parts
can they be put together?

collage and bricolage …
how do we assemble ourselves?
and why do we have
so many parts?

03.11

in the heart of a latvian forest
stand two ikons
no one kneels before them
but they exist nonetheless

the air is heavy
with the prayer ineffable

if some day one hiker
makes it to
the heart of these dense woods
before which ikon
will he kneel?

upon the brink of the
journey's resolution
will he be paralyzed
by indecision?

03.12

an indecipherable smear
is all that's left behind
that old uniformity
was pure imposture
beneath those surfaces
nothing was as it seemed

at the middle of the journey
inversion is required
but the center point
is hard to locate—
there is nothing there

03.13

the ubiquity of
contradictions implies
binaries and
forces of equilibrium

there is always
room for another
element in the equation
variable upon variable

the equation is not
meant to be solved

03.14

the great ones are
assembled together
and they blether in unison

i scramble up
the mountainside
to escape the cacophony

their self-important voices
drone on and on as i leave
the sound and the
fury far behind

i'll trace these words
on the side of a sheer
cliff wall—
let the elements
wear them away

to the blank slate prepared
by the illusion of time
we return again and again

only those who are silent
have anything to say

03.15

epistemological guerrillas
wage secret battles
their tactics
have evolved surely
from the beginning until now
even though there
was no beginning
and there is no now

you can hear their advance
when you stop listening
you can see them out of
the corner of your eye

if you look directly at them
they disappear
leaving behind only
the fading sound of laughter

03.16

what unsung song relates
the journey of a hero?
is the pace of the hero steady?
he takes his leisure
along the path

perhaps he knows
there's no hurry
or maybe he needed to
dance out a calf cramp
then sate himself
with exotic liquors

he needs no maps
he intuits
there's no such thing
as being lost

03.17

the dilution of pleasure
has become habitual
life is now just
slow decay for most
most grow inured
to the constant odor of
their own decomposition

secular self-mortification
rules the day
let intense sensations
subvert reigning orthodoxies

03.18

peculiar noises and
the viscera stretch taut
the tone is one of
apprehension
uncertainty begets uncertainty
but the alternative is worse

the totalizing immurement
of certainty—

better the spasmodic dance
of the aleatory

03.19

what elements resonate with
platonic perfection in this
now-degraded empyrean?

their essence has been
defiled and perverted
develop some new
alchemical procedure

there is a gradual purification
though it too is imperfect
asymptotically tending
toward a state
inconsistent with
the city of man

weight must be cast
off until all
that's left floats up and away

03.20

in the shadow of
the large rock we wait
excessive haste
will not do here
our bodies will know
when the time is right
only then will we
begin to inch forward

for now we recline
and wait for the music
to work some change in us

03.21

and there is a continual
estrangement
cones of disquiet
rise up before us
expanding shapes
covered in perfectly
smooth frictionless skin

they cannot be scaled
or circumvented
faster and faster
we change direction
and rabbit off
until another cone
rises up before us

this is the great distraction
i close my eyes
i walk leisurely ahead
not one phantom
cone obstructs
the vision of my inner eye

03.22

is there a theory of devolution?
gradual or abrupt?

i can hear the tempo change
as we race toward the precipice
or slouch habitually toward
some entropic mire

who will disengage from the
city of man?

and what's the
ignominious slide
of the species to me anyway?

03.23

‘imperium’
i hear a woman
enunciate carefully

confused voices hail
equinoctial inversion
brisk air penetrates the
inner fibers of the soul

in the distance a bell
tolls periodically
the byways are all but deserted

a solitary walker presses on
toward a destination unknown

03.24

all is noise and confusion
but with a driving rhythm
and middle european accent

what is it tugging the careless
stroller toward?

city of dis city of man
the gross physical plane
whose so-called virtues
are meted out using a
byzantine system of
weights and measures

the very air is filled
with sinister particles
they will blind you if
you continue on

it is permitted to rewind
there are always other paths

the better route is
seldom direct
but it is always
marked by silence

03.25

this limited range
of movement
is spawned by an
imperfect lexicon
certain key terms are repeated
and we are left
seeking patterns
attempting to press
some tenuous
chaos into the silicon
form of progress

there is a film over the eyes
and most will blunder into an
imperceptible web
of silken threads

extrication is a delicate process
find the clear line that
bisects confinement
it is a passageway
though a narrow one

03.26

it is a repeated phrase
perhaps only
within my own head

i parse it out but
the meaning is vague

there is a longing
a longing for a state of
perfection incompatible
with the human condition

if tunes and tempos
are not debased
the ears of hearers are

what then is
the purpose of music?

03.27

i think about latin prefixes
i wonder about the differences
between movement
to
from
around
across
through
beyond

there is some peripatetic
slouching that carries one—
forward?

the illusion of progress
is pernicious
many other illusions
are subordinate to it
baroque structure of
intertwined mendacities

explosion of percussion
opens up in my head
there is an image
trying to form but i see
only mass confusion
masked by a surety of purpose
at odds with anything
we dare call truth

04.01

look for
pattern symmetry repetition

some things are cyclical
others arranged in triads

all studies will be
meaningless in the end
the search for wisdom
will yield nought

there on the corner of
a busy city street
a silent tear scars a
carbon cheek
balthazar holds out
a dirty hand

04.02

we always return to
variable climatic conditions
much to our peril
repetition grows tiresome

but what of time's
fruitful symmetry?

the voices always return
subtle at first
in unknown languages
we try to translate

but rapidly changing
temperatures
defeat our sense apparatus

could there be
meaning in these
meaningless phrases
repeated as they are by
bored monotonous voices?

04.03

flowers have died and
birds grow agitated
they long to fly up
out of this valley

the solitary walker
grows weary
of low elevations

the walker seeks literal assent
he knows the falsity
of spiritual metaphor

everything appears flat
but angles of incidence vary

hypnagogic song will rouse
the walker from his reverie
and his pace will quicken

somewhere beyond
the horizon
the mountain of the
mind beckons

04.04

indecipherable names
and a premonitory vision
malignant forces abound
only the interstices offer
a slim chance at transcendence

the residue of some
new secular
bacchanal is all around

heavy traffic in the city of dis
frequent fatal collisions

the smart ones grow lean
and slip between the cracks

engines of avarice
keep running
cacophony and black smoke
nullify the senses

denizens of dis collide
particles in a chamber

citizens are drawn to
communal dining halls
by an irresistible scent

smell of their own
flesh roasting

04.05

they are inventing an
immortality machine

rusted metal golem
waiting to be reanimated
by the copious
spittle of human folly

04.06

grim adagios but
we hobble on just the same
others race past
emitting a chemical stench

there is a change at work
not just mechanical alteration
but genuine transformation

the movement slows
but continues indefinitely
color drains away
and moisture evaporates

the fastest ones are
now desiccated skeletons
all medals and ribbons
now ossified nostalgia

the races are forgotten
the old man walks away
from the remains of
a finish line

04.07

what is this metaphysical
topography?
does place presuppose
movement to or from?

very quickly tone
timbre tempo alter
skewing our perspective

profound sense compression

directions bifurcate
and recombine
forming helical structures

thought-spirals conjure
myths of ascent
but also descent

reality replicates time's
frantic dreamscape
but its tempo is
wrong all wrong

the vision has been
refracted through
some strange medium

a minor truth shimmers
tantalizingly
in the distance then fades away

04.08

the shape shifters
have descended
from the northern lands
geometric juxtapositions
could hold the key
to arcane languages
and pregnant symbols

every nothing is different

orderly minds place data
in appropriate quadrants
the flash returns to its source
illumination ceases

04.09

somewhere the ancient
songs are still sung
forgotten mournful
chord sequences
precipitate from the clouds

the patriarchs are silent

now voices issue from
the smooth cheeks of youth
no words worth hearing
will be uttered now

fearful resonance
gives way to the
impotent squeaks of the now

04.10

green expanse divided into
units of roughly equal area
the priest caste is out
taking measurements

an accumulation of facts
is not the same as truth
the wordless incantation
activates cognitive valence

dimensions and shapes
pale before spiritual ratios

04.11

a puff of air
first or last breath?
they are the same

04.12

the illusion of peace
is a fearful sideshow
under the calliope's
harsh discord
the freaks
don their disguises

everyone will be called
to their table
as the cymbals and
gongs increase
the intensity of
their deafening summons

a solitary walker
will be seen ascending
the hill behind
the dining tent
where the unlucky ones
become macabre delicacies

04.13

again and again we hear
voices from the northern lands
how to interpret these
strange dialects?

the tone is monitory
the message dark confusion
to the source we must trek

early we tramp on
hoar frost and
struggle to breathe
this rarefied air

burning our lungs so
we cannot cry out
in anger or in supplication

still the voices goad
us on though
we cannot know
their meaning

04.14

i come upon this
sacred number again and
try to suss out its meaning
if any

filter noise and confusion

temperature drops
precipitously and
low notes rumble
in the viscera

still i contemplate
the number and
seek out its presence
around me

suddenly it is everywhere and
its multiples too they multiply

is there division? and if
the parts are adjoining
are they not one?

04.15

indecision returns
the length of the
road was a factor
as was its serial pavement

some fell into a natural stride
but progress was not
a relevant term

others halted and
some turned back
a few hacked through
the brush
and formed new paths
paths that led to nowhere

one sat comfortably
in the hills
above the network of roadways

the sound of his
laughter echoes on

04.16

an image will form
upon the surface
lines traced faintly
grow bold

patterns emerge but
shift more rapidly
than imperfect perception
can assimilate
or explicate

a constant tone
finally stops
just as the hearer
approaches the brink
of madness

moment of dread
lucidity fades
as the mind is filled with
the perfection of emptiness

04.17

word repeated like a curse
then i realize it's my name
at least one of them

passersby hurl abuse at me
my pace neither
waxes nor wanes

malediction i think to myself
i project a blue image
the barking of the hordes fades
to a most harmonious silence

some strive for immortality
through taoist postures
and calisthenics

i repeat the name
both sacred and profane
and lose myself in the rhythms
of my own silent speech

04.18

continuous ritual left us
with hoarse voices
and bad knees
the forms of worship vary
but all the idols are false

altars perverted by
the reification
of unreliable sense data

the quiet is ruptured by a siren
whose piercing
summons brings
all the wrong worshippers

the climate in the village
they abandoned
is much improved

04.19

the city's supernatural ideal
has been degraded
now the denizens ply
their bestial ways

and savagery concentrates
gross physical vectors criss-
cross and enweb the city

04.20

corrugation disrupts
the cognitive texture
now i have nothing
to go on
the music has stopped
or been drowned out
by the dubious
industry of man

everywhere motors
and hammers are busy
the sound of birdsong
hovers faintly above it all
i want birds to come
down to the walk
but the sound of man
repels them

what direction
shall i haul this broken body?
is there a pocket of peace
amidst the din
where birds might
light around me thinking
perhaps i'm some
post-apocalyptic saint francis?

04.21

listen carefully
for words of wisdom
the deafening noise is
gobbledygook not proverbs

and when this web of
clichés is unraveled
who will find solace?

record the words and
play them backwards
do they make a little
more sense this way?

04.22

in the lowlands
the wind blows
variations in elevation
produce unpredictable effects
irreconcilables seem to
meet for a moment

intensified hues overlap
muted tones
warm and cool intermingle
as they touch bare skin
there is a sense of urgency

the lackadaisical walker
continues his desultory stroll
as cautious optimism
gives way to jaunty cynicism

the washed out façade
of the temple can just
be perceived against
the colorless sky

the sun's intensity is temporary
in the shade a chill descends

there's a faint change in
the air's shifting particles
the energy we seek is subtle

sensitive ones feel its
constant presence

04.23

two pistons fire rapidly
their rhythm seems to
speak the name tristan
or is it *triste*?

an overwhelming sadness
at a loss so great
it cannot be quantified

when quantity is the
epistemological
coin of the realm

ennui seeps into everything
locomotion grows perfunctory
consumption continues apace

sleepwalkers populate
the grim landscape
but the dreamscape will wake
a select few with its
riot of color

04.24

in the nighttime valley
a circular procession
winds around a fire
with each revolution
the walkers near the fire

lost in their own monologues
—ego-enslaved—
each begins to hum
his own insipid tune

the flames pull them closer
as if they long to silence
and purify the promenaders

as the first bodies
begin to burn
an orchestra strikes up

the burning walkers
dance spasmodically
a chorus of screams
in lively harmony

the rancid smoke
from their worthless bodies
transforms into frankincense

whose sweet perfume
settles over the valley
as a most fitting
silence returns to the land

04.25

a strangely familiar instrument
invents new languages
eerie sounds
communicate pure feeling
bypassing the twin quagmires
of cognition and analysis

the sharpness of the
morning air
is scarcely mitigated by
subtle grunts of supplication
should these formless prayers
ever be answered
a torrent of tears
shall flow without surcease

04.26

preternatural memory returns
signaled by a single
high-pitched tone
personality and
subjectivity fade

a strange image bank
is made available
sight and sound at first
refuse to synchronize
but gradually the
postlapsarian mind
ceases its stuttering

colored shapes break
down into
atmospheric pixels and
sound explodes into
an infinitude of waves

though nothing we can see or
hear is strictly identifiable
there is a beauty

04.27

understanding is embodied
in an apparition
he who would understand
is emboldened by
a singular vision

the so-called
progression of time
forecloses the imagination

sight and vision are
not the same thing
though they may
be the opposite

in the occident we will
now communicate
exclusively through
contradictory verses

i waked from sleep as if
from another world
i walked and when
i saw i knew
i carried within me the
very dreamscape

05.01

toward extinction

walls close in and
the blind feel frantically
for chink or gap

each world seems real at first
illusion is sustained until
the phantasmagoria
becomes apparent

no new language
can articulate it
nor arcane spells disarm it

yet the sound of song
is discernable
its source lies just beyond
the wall of flame

05.02

what light there is
is refracted through
fluid spheres

anticipation is
dull and diffuse

dulcet eastern notes
are driven out by
the frenetic noise of
mechanical menace

locomotion is a struggle
against myriad ambient forces

magnetic particles deep within
the earth produce
chthonic forces

this dark compression
seems inescapable
somewhere a voice cries out
calling for light

05.03

wet black leaves
carpet the path
the bedlamites howl
and gibber
they are warding off
invisible demons

that you cannot see them
doesn't prove they don't exist
the rational mind drowns in
a sea of negatives

05.04

direction is reversed
under the influence
of the swan
there will be novelty
in this surfeit of sense data

the perceiver has altered
his angle of observation
and high-frequency
tones spur him on

neatly arranged
domiciles are abandoned—
yet another failed civilization

rumbles of mechanical
life in the distance
warn of the latest attempt
to build a civilization

the walker strides resolutely
away from the noise
into the perfect silence

05.05

bursts of fire
transfigure the colorless sky
and i read my history in
the backside of a mirror

the walker sheds his pack
and continues on

05.06

a group of mechanical demons
generates dust and noise
while the hordes are frog-
marched into the
dense woods of nostalgia

a tinkling piano plays
an insipid tune for
undiscriminating ears

voices meanwhile drone on
lecturing into the void

the mystics have
stopped their ears
in the distance a walker hears
a perfunctory round
of applause

05.07

dust filth rubbish muck
the walker wades through
an impasto of decomposing
organic matter—
memento mori

he longs to merge with it
let the journey come to an end
end the pointless exhaustion
dissolve into the
earth and cease

he walks on

05.08

the outlines of this reality have
taken on an unpleasant
sharpness

momentary reprieve
of the mind
creates a landscape of
perfect layered color

the sonic dimension
lifts the veil
and the false reality is
pulled aside for the moment

the inner eye assembles
the vision
an explosion of
synesthetic perfection
guides the walker toward bliss

05.09

three towers smudge
and merge
rain and rage bring confusion
the mind wanders
down dark cerebral alleys

still the rain falls

the walker returns to a
road he's walked before
landscape now earth tones
russet gold brown
predominating

sound of three similar songs
weaves itself into one
a tenuous peace settles

05.10

many heads bob to the surface
they are coming up for air
they drink it
they drink the air
until it makes them sick

i dive deep without
fear of drowning
the air was drowning me
now i breathe freely

sight and sound are refracted
through this alchemical
medium
could any eyes or ears
withstand this terrible beauty?

05.11

the pattern is relentless
counterpoint constructed
structures
built block by block

asymmetric goad startles
the senses into a frenzy
sound inebriates and
motion follows

choreographic feedback loop
a celtic question:
the dancer from the dance?

perfection of verbless motion
interior sounds and steps
explode across time and space

as if they existed

05.12

everything begins to recede
and the few remaining objects
are outlined clearly
stark geometric shapes
in the growing void

everything dissolves into
shapes angles lines

just atoms now—
combined and recombined
chance or changing order

of the countless atoms
a few million or so
will linger and malinger
around the perimeter
molecular wallflowers
at the cosmic dance

05.13

spontaneous composition
disparate notes are mapped
onto physical compounds

for a moment it's almost as
if the physical world existed

three tang-era flutes bring me
back to the spirit realm
mad monks seek immortality
through chanting and elixirs

the walker heads for the hills
to join the long-
dead immortals

a harmonic triptych
colors the cliff walls
their song will transcend
time and space

05.14

in subterranean blackness
the walker wends his way

all earth now
an abandoned mine

dark dwarves axed axiology
they carried away
the last traces of ore

in these empty shafts
and tunnels
the walker finds the bones of
souls forced to work with
pick shovel cart

the bones rest calmly
in the silence now

the dwarves are gone
now they work their
dark mischief in
boardroom and duma

the walker emerges
from the black mineshaft
into dazzling light

he sees before him
a series of blinding peaks

05.15

far from the machinations
of the dwarves

alpine herbs and tart berries
sustain him as he
makes his ascent

the temperature drops
but the walker's constant
motion keeps him warm

humanity is a virulent strain
scattering its dread
spores of malignancy

the earth breaks out in buboes

sounds of grim cello and viola
welcome patches of
intensely saturated color

has the walker entered
the place of the dead?
or is it some amorphous
vestibule?

for many the sinews
have atrophied
black necrotic limbs
stacked at right angles
cromlechs commemorating
those who stopped moving

the way of the walker
is singular
few who hear his music will
survive its potent spell

most will fall with
twisted limbs
frozen in mockeries of prayer

05.16

the forest is a sickly
shade of green
mottled in places with
excremental brown
it is fighting off a virus and
awaiting the arrival
of the walker

in the diseased canopy—
though no one's
there to see it—
pockets of light

05.17

just faded remnants
every road is degraded

but as temporal
fiction evaporates
a small red tree appears
then another and another

improbable color in
a colorless world
in the distance scarlet
blurs and blobs
against the gelid lifeless air

all the music had to fade and
die down to pure
silence before
the music of the spheres
could be heard

and everything contained
within itself its opposite

and every walker
everywhere paused and
listened

05.18

delicate sounds
penetrate the skin
without leaving a mark
the body is slowly transformed

unseen energies
become tangible
this is the existence outside
time and space

cracked pavement and
the noise of humanity
signal a return to the world
the walker will carry
this vague memory
and bear within himself
a discreet mark

higher and lower
orders interwoven
no communication
without contradiction

05.19

the movement of
molecules slows
the field is frozen hard
every atom and every particle
strain under the cold
bloodless sun

equine hair screams
through feline viscera
monitory sonnets
speak of the cold—
an old god from the old times
seeking victims or at
least propitiation

he blows hard and
fills the air with
ice crystals whose
deathly beauty
and pure structural perfection
cannot be seen by
the frozen hordes

05.20

music was anticipated yet
somehow unexpected

jaunty rhythms conceal
secret words

the sun's shifting chiaroscuro
provides only
intermittent warmth

vibration is ubiquitous and
subtle frequencies
can always be detected

the music is colored by
ambient conditions

and always we struggle
for the meaning behind it

there are words whose
meanings can never be known

pronouncing them strikes
fear in the hearer's heart

what perfect sequence
of notes will combat
the chill engendered
by the secret name?

05.21

small berries shiny and black
their juices are frozen but
still contain their fell toxins

starving dark-eyed juncos
will not approach them

malignant energies suspended
in grim potentiality

05.22

automatism is rampant and
all this busy-ness seems
organized and controlled by
some benevolent director

but the subtle scent of sewer
gives pause
efficiency's martial beat
sickens some

bodies seem limber when
executing rote flexing
and bending
but unexpected moves reveal
painfully frozen joints

work to dance against the beat
unlock hidden motion
kinetic transcendence

05.23

bold strokes etch the cliff wall
three strange pictograms will
be seen by few or none

who will seek this elevation?
good citizens cannot breathe
in air as thin as this

the mad poets have fled
the crowded towns and cities
they dwell in transient
structures
well above the foothills

when the moon is up
their flutes dance
in the morning light
empty bottles glitter

05.24

the return of
predictable motion
raises the specter of dead ends
the road seems to exist as a fact
but without painful
concentration
its contours blur and shift

some walkers let
thought recede
through some lethargic magic
they proceed

05.25

what comes this way?
vague shape but
seen in ancient memory

two metaphysical tramps
pass a cigarette back and forth
light snow begins to fall

the image somehow persists
ethereal kingdom

if steps exist they are now
just ruined stone fragments
nowhere to go

just ringing bells that might be
auditory hallucinations

with the two tramps we wait
everyone waits

05.26

mystical landscape
trees burning against
celestial striations

fire and air are
consumed within
one another

underfoot the earth
heaves and groans
somewhere ahead

is a riverbank and
the water's ceaseless
flow contains all time

05.27

false voices chatter on
speaking of a cut-rate paradise

sickly sweet voices
prove emetic
was this the purification?

now in the empty space
left by their departed heaven

i can just make out
three dark circles
i drown in their beauty and

wait to be reborn

06.01

last ditch effort to
communicate
disorienting energy suffuses
this space-time—left
with only questions now

that might be called a
true statement
voices hold no answers
just as well—questions
might nourish

every answer the
same grim endpoint
the voices have
no meaning—that
is their beauty

06.02

the systems rumble
and compete
hear them and try to count

for some mechanical otherness
generates comforting noises
for others a terrifying
metallic lullaby

four systems five systems
six systems eight systems
components assemble
and reassemble

the edges of geometric
objects blur
and the colors of these now
irregular shapes grow muted
and underneath the
sound of the systems
the song of tree frogs
in the distance

06.03

motion slows almost to a stop
strange crackling sounds and
bold striations of
bright and dark

faint talismanic voices chant
against molecular torpor

did something warm the belly
of the poet? his flute sounds

06.04

songs against happy endings—
that's an appropriate start
we are dulled by
repetition now
discordant rumblings rise
above the wind

somewhere a taped
voice is played backwards
vibrations of the
right frequency
heat the skin and
quash anxiety

for now disorientation
must be used to advantage
bad directions only
appear to mislead

06.05

three songs which
hearers struggle
to tell apart

beginning and end
are not
relevant concepts

not to mention
duration

once-stately trees
reduced
to intersecting lines

a great thirst
came upon me

slowly color
seeped back
into the dream

time cracked open to
reveal
a compact vision

whether of past or future
isn't clear and
probably doesn't matter

06.06

what is this ubiquitous
discoloration?
place of distortion
the usual confusion
of solid objects
and predictable angles
uniform surfaces
are acted upon
by unknown forces

three men carrying
quadrilaterals
uneasy procession as
fading humanity submits to
the final geometry

06.07

black oxygen suggests
a thickening of the air

rarefied frozen vapors
are gone for the moment

inchoate forces now
just detectable

the beginning had
not yet come

subterranean energies
are at work

all that's visible
above the ground
is just a symptom

straight lines and
right angles retreat

06.08

strange carols from
flat affectless voices
conjure stupor

gradual decline

sporadic blotches
of strange colors
mar muted gray beauty

a tight orbit requires
increasing sharpness of vision

perception's edges grow jagged
there are no lines
only points

06.09

urgent percussion and
a sequence of wrong turns

cognitive bifurcations
mirrored
in seemingly random
movements
oscillations between
the four colors

objects tessellate endlessly
molecular deviations
combinations are
difficult to avoid

the energy undergoes
constant change

06.10

faint scent of vegetal decay
and the memory of
anthropomorphic flowers
gives way to poured concrete
saturated with cold rain water

all is juxtaposition

06.11

light and sound in
architectonic layers

invisible barrier

air heavy as lead
prevents access
to the empyrean

consuming some
imperfect vapors
listening for change

the sound is blue
and layered
dull force blocks
the light within

terrible effulgence
remains potential
some light cannot
be viewed directly

sudden sharp odor
—not unpleasant—
brings back the
shifting temporalities
of this penumbra

06.12

somewhere the sound of
a prayer in reverse

water makes
fine rivulets—
elemental subtlety
as two muted colors
engage in what could
be the final struggle

06.13

noncommittal cosmic
gestures add up
not in the sense of make sense
they don't

meaningless accumulation
like all accumulation
manufactured
necessity deceives

the shrug of equanimity says
das ist mir egal
a seductive voice repeats
spazieren
          spazieren
                    spazieren

06.14

painfully beautiful surfaces
insistent sounds and
tachycardia
then release

subtle expressions of
deflated desire
this is the metaphysical
detumescence

what grim realities reside
beneath the gaudy surface?

06.15

air oppresses and
elemental imbalances
suggest the presence
of a threshold

passing through or
across or over
or beyond

the cold prickle
of intense heat
prepares the body
for strange rituals

the room that's not a room
holds pain pleasure madness
in equal measure

06.16

unexpected lines of
resistance open
dead silence between
vocal explosions
inspires moderate dread

path worn almost
to nonexistence
leads to a sign reading
chamber number two

the number two implies
the existence of
other chambers
does the french *chambre*
offer a place of rest?
or six loaded chambers
poised against time's temple?

or the other roulette?
red or black?
odd or even?

yes

06.17

uncategorizable sounds and
unrecognizable shapes
foster labored breathing

there must be one point
on one line in one plane
about which we can
know one thing

or one note in one sequence—
could its true tone be heard
by ears in this shadow realm?

there must be a light
somewhere
and an object for us
to reside within this shadow

06.18

dread electrons orbit
their recombinations
transform matter

psychic disorientation follows
highly charged fluids course
through composite bodies

destroying and renewing

06.19

is it a coming together
or a simultaneity?
are independent phenomena
occurring in parallel?

is union presupposed
by consonance?

the minor chords
are strong now
and limited visibility
demands intuitive
navigation

nonparallel lines must
at some point cross

movement is slow
with senses dulled
by time

only simple shapes
are forming now
but
complexity's robust potential
will be activated

06.20

the spherical form requires no
apparatus of walking
said timaeus

such a form is limited
to circular movements
with no deviation permitted

this was thought to
be perfection
the walker embodies
the imperfect

there are no perfect shapes
the surface of the
sphere is rough
and irregular when
viewed up close

only when kept at a
great distance
can this orb exist

06.21

just fragments held together
by invisible forces

can a message be received
that was never sent?

apparently meaningful
utterances
sporadically surface in this
sea of noise

just random elemental
combinations
that serve some brief function
then recombine

the random itself
pulses out of time
drawing the receptive into its
attenuated energy

06.22

elevation's subtle deception
begins to work its
strange magic
particles of energy begin
to descend all around

ambient softness
mutes the voices
and all momentum is banished
words fade and smear
an unbearable brightness is
contained within the bleakness

the rhythm of the
dance is subtle
but perceptible
time's laughable progression
stutters within this
transtemporal now

the notes grow lively now
all movement restored
there is a quickening
and all forces are synchronized
in this sharp cold moment

06.23

miasma leaks from
ruptured preconceptions
gelatinous negative energy
clings to everything
all surfaces slick and
smelling of raw sewage

the way to hyperion
is charted by a confusion
of astronomical roadmaps
that refuse to refold
they are too thin
to be used as blankets
against the cold
in this vagrant alleyway
but may be found
to serve some purpose

06.24

light passes through
four prisms
as animal spirits achieve
a dense minerality

a subtle sickness sets in
total uniformity reigns
either disaster or
boredom awaits

06.25

a sequence of names
is uttered by a
cantor clad in metallic
monk's robes
names name the unnamable

every light peels back the skin
until the juicy flesh beneath
dries and withers

mad monks and defrocked
doppelgangers seek some
powerful incantation whose

words reside maddeningly
just beyond meaning

06.26

rhythmic percussion raises
the tribal fallacy—
movements dictated
metonymically

some will wander off
under cover of shadow
far from the fertile delta's
densely populated plain

solitary souls ascend
rocky paths where the
drumbeats fade to nothing
a tentative flute sounds

06.27

letters rearrange themselves
words can offer no
stable meaning

even a recognizable
series of tones
is in the end and is
in the beginning
a meaningless sequence

strong forces are
unexpected and
novel information
must be extracted
from the surrounding noise

then
          discarded
it is the noise
          the noise itself
and the jumble of letters
          glyphs
                    ciphers

no meaning no message
but a tiny force
opening sensations
twisting perceptions

07.01

a powerful rhythmic drive
pushes everything forward
we reside for the moment
in some future past and
all color is contained
within an infinitely dark patch
or a flash of brilliant light

the mind's prism separates
and distills
senses are corrupted
and unreliable
we have been pulled out of
the now
and our essence is scattered
over nonexistent
timescapes

sterility dictates our
inarticulate mumblings
the absence of a shadow
leaves behind a hole
could this emptiness
be a passageway?

07.02

the rhythmic avian dance
has been forestalled by
powerful forces

dense empty clusters
unfold their nothingness

huddled near a fire
a woman in motley
smokes a pipe and waits

in this stationary dance
expectation rules

winter's harsh geometry
is ascendant

when the music starts again
we will go
where it takes us

07.03

the sky is freshly limned
just another stage set
treacly music and
happy endings

microscopic tears reveal
a dull gray beneath the
manufactured cerulean

a solitary observer
sometimes sees
through the gaps

and one isolated
listener hears
the sound of discord

there is also the
faint sound of scraping
and there are yawns

a piece of rotting fruit is
crushed on the pavement
ding-dong

somewhere a damaged cell
divides and spreads
tra-la-la

07.04

radioactivity's toxic spores
infect the pia mater
paralysis sets in

who are these
walking homunculi?

radiation from an
unknown source
transmits its rays

some control mechanism
will become jammed
            locks cease
to function

a slow drip at first
then the flow
            unchanneled

all forces will be unleashed
the intransitive revolution
has begun

07.05

somber tones of phase change
can disintegration
be far behind?

fragile beauty holds the
imperfect perception
in precarious balance

all is filtered through a layer
transparent but transformative

a moment's concentration
shatters the brittle isinglass
that sheltered the soul
and distorted the vision

keen perception now
and hypersensitivity to
pain and pleasure
especially when
they come together

07.06

a subtle moiré in
the fabric of the universe
ominous pulse of
bulbous striations

we are on the cusp

warring forces create
a band of turbulence
superimposed exactly
upon the path

gasses circulate within
intercellular spaces
no motion no sound
precision grows
from silence

07.07

another triad
a voice describes three places
somewhere to the north
and to the east

a woman's voice offers
directions there
but the leaves are
curled and withered and
a journey seems ill-advised

the ambient moisture
is oppressive
moss and lichen
cover every surface

i seek a secret ally
a shadowy figure
warms itself by a fire
i lurk in darkness and
wait to hear the music

07.08

once the bamboo's brittle
winter leaves were silver—
a sickly yellow has set in

what atlantean submersion
has enveloped us? and why
this gruesome color palette?

07.09

reason's poison inertia
calls for an awakening
wake into the dream
not from it

there are five doors
in the dream and
we are instructed to
knock at each in turn

the door creaks open
whose face?
whose voice?
a blessing or a curse?

and how will we
know the difference?

07.10

strange strains come
from the middle distance
elemental chord progressions
with a shadowy aura

but just at the edges of hearing
the sound of
unidentifiable birds
and a song of praise

there is a lightness now
as if the weight has been
emptied out of everything

the leaden forms of the
shadow realm become ethereal

07.11

i hear accompaniment
but accompaniment to what?

cool wet air is everywhere
a pungent scent of cooking
food lingers in space

and still this music—
unwholesome tempo
posits pointless urgency

loop of movement
leaves us nowhere

the circumscribed space
—though empty—
may contain some clue

07.12

collector of substances
stares into the sky
intently

the sun must have risen
but it cannot be seen

the planets the collector
ponders most are
mercury and saturn
and sometimes venus

lunar and planetary influences
—heavy concepts—

the collector stumbles on
narrowly missing a
disintegrating cigar butt
with his well-shod right foot

07.13

some dual change is at work
bright rays of pure light
pierce the dull atmosphere

evaporation transforms
the ambient miasma

strings vibrate at
discernable frequencies
and the energy passes
into matter animating it

hot breath of mystic
ecstasy spurs us on

dervishes trapped within
atrophied bodies await
the onslaught of
charged particles

07.14

slowly the feeling comes
like gentle fingers
palpating spheres of glass

high-pitched tones make
visible sine waves
through the lower atmosphere

each frequency wave
transmits a different color

this is not dissonance
but the tightly woven
pattern of the random

07.15

translucent substances
alter the quality of light
somewhere a device is
being built to trap the light
and transform it into
dark energy

dark particles will
bombard all bodies
and motion will undergo
an irresistible deceleration

some bodies will rock
gently and wait
wait until they become
their own source of light

07.16

sinister polkas deceive
feet stamping on asphalt
marching is not walking

wait for plucked strings
and rhythmic humming
subtle passageways exist

vestigial shadows
of two wreaths
mark some path undetectable
by most sets of eyes

wait behind the shamelessly
naked trunk of the sycamore
marchers tramp loudly past

the solitary walker slips into
the woods drawn toward the
sounds of faint humming
and bottles opening

07.17

nature's false avatar
constructs a web

its beauty and
complexity imprison

misleading chants
hypnotize

nonsense syllables
convey strange meaning

this wordless conversation
generates color

shifting pigments
glow with energy

new sounds emerge

07.18

ululating chants of
mad monks
open a rift in the wall
now visions of another world
will assault the unready

prohibitions abound and
repetition drives some
to despair

invisible maps are
laid over the territory

subtle shifting patterns
are found in the rubbish
cast out by nonbelievers

07.19

darkness? or just
shifting patterns of light
they say these are the waters
yet all is dry—
a sea of asphalt
under constant shadow

elemental copulation
as ground and sky
merge grayly—
a joyless coupling
announces sterility

it lacks the fire
          the heat
                    the light

07.20

time's ubiquitous outspreading
has left it attenuated to
the point of transparency

pleasure will awaken every cell
some bodies will float in
the cosmic medium

this lightness is like
another dimension
above and beyond
or deep within

paces quicken and
a green feeling
seeps into
everything

07.21

north star rising
one walker's energy
returns to the
upper atmosphere

good and evil collide
forming a great
convection current
storms will ensue

07.22

some pay homage but
memory is a form of forgetting

the pure energy though
transformed is constant

listen for strange frequencies
and phantom transmissions

some music was always present
though seldom heard

delicate shifting tones derive
from some rotation

pure sound of shapes
and colors
can never mislead

07.23

symphony composed around
an imagined note
sculpture carved from
the malleable substance
of pure oxygen

poem whose name
cannot be pronounced

07.24

chimes will sound
go

air morphs into a solid
taut with energy
go

rising and falling notes
major chords and
minor chords
mallets fall on space
go

percussion explodes
scattering its particles
signs will appear
strangled horns try to sound
go

07.25

hot light and cold air mingle
some will shiver and burn
untrimmed wicks
burn brightly

many lines converge
and intersect
as a bell tolls insistently
followed by low notes
at quick tempos

another city in its death throes
or so a melodic convergence
announces dispassionately

there is beauty in decline
and necessity too
verdigris covers an
arcane symbol

old symbols no one recognizes
or understands—powerful
new symbols abound

brilliant new surfaces
conceal the void beneath
but suck meaning
from worshippers

a flat surface struggles
to expand
into another dimension
all shapes harbor the potential

07.26

deep in the woods
four strings resonate
the source of this sound
is uncertain

low frequencies form spirals
diameters increase
exponentially

at a distance
subtle waves exert
subliminal influence

far from the forest
someone might follow
the curves of the pattern
and work backward somehow
to the source

07.27

once again sounds
from the north
primitive rhythms

skin-clad traveling
musicians are drawn
to powerful
magnetic forces

before civilization
and after
bards will quaff
strong liquor
and translate
sharp geometries

shamans eat angles and
vomit colored dreams
northern flutes
stitch together
occident and orient

only frequent use will
soften this coarse fabric

08.01

notes but not on a staff
will form an open-
textured map

often comes the
sound of a flute
the sound returns
again and again
and each time it is
easier to hear
having moved closer
without realizing

we didn't notice the map
it was beneath our feet

its two dimensions could only
support the weight of a third
not explain or predict it

it sought to describe what was
beneath it and to conceal it

but now organ blasts
drown out
the flute and somewhere in the
suffocating ether the circle
attempts to square itself

08.02

scrambled voices
sing terrifying lullabies
face north and plug your ears

just beneath the
surface of the earth
uniformed trolls operate
the timeworks
greasing its cogs with
the rendered fat
of those who stopped to listen

face north—do not listen
but hear faint sounds from
far beyond the black noise

face north and walk
scan bleak horizons
for the place where
colored peaks burst
through the earth
and ascend toward
space

face north

08.03

an organized inquiry
starves the soul

visible forces are
insidious distractions

who will cultivate
unseen agencies?

and who bids
farewell to sanity?

a dim figure packs
pen and flute then
silently slips away

08.04

denizens of the city
of the plain
hear bold pronouncements
and repetitious chants

some have fled the dense
superimposition of shapes
they linger at each
distinct form

far down in the city below
horn blasts can just be heard
but on the winding
paths of ascent

flutes will sound

08.05

throngs in the city
footsteps
          shouts
                    motors

what song penetrates
chaotic noise?

solitude is hypothetical
yet all walking is solitary

somewhere restorative cordials
smooth the jagged edges of
space's messy immensity

08.06

terrible drumming
from the inside
urgent message
confinement within
forms and shapes

some force would
free itself from
the dead weight of
instantiation

robot crows guard the grave
solemn strings distract
with syrupy passages

colored flutes will sound
prussian blue
          prasine
                    heliotrope

these colored sounds send
fissures through the
outer forms
the surfaces are cracking

08.07

dull planes merge and double
until new sounds emerge
ever-expanding two
dimensionality
is pierced by seemingly
random notes

these tiny holes might
form some pattern
when the notes join
a gnomon breaks loose

the deep saturation of its
new color is absolute
such purity rests uneasily
with geometry's apostates

08.08

who lives in hidden cities?
invisible habitations exist
in some concealed dimension

in such places not one
calculates the volume
of a sphere

energy is transmitted
directly and
instantaneously

altitude may be a
seductive fiction
but

between the seashore
and the mountaintop
lies only hostile territory

08.09

on the pavement an apple core
and a faded stencil impart
profound knowledge to some
deranged observer

there are messages
to be deciphered

leaves of tea
grounds of coffee
major and minor arcana
warm viscera

mysteries seek mediation
but who can tell apart
the charlatan from
the shaman?

08.10

who thinks existence is
predicated upon language?
and what distortions
govern motion?

following any path to
its conclusion
leads to madness
or mystic revelation

experts lecture and
repetition strives
for dogmatism but
through time
meaning leaks away

every word has a shape
they might be put together
in various combinations

self-reflexive utterances
value enunciation
over elucidation

words combine and
recombine but
do the speakers of
these words exist?

08.11

shining black stones
and low notes

narrow passageway
through space and time

tinny percussion and
voices of indignation

give way to a
metaphysical calliope

don't let it trap you
in the passageway

emerge from every passage
as if reborn

slick with blood and
blinded by light

soon you'll learn words
and how to walk

08.12

would elements be
commanded?
two solids collide and
air is forced through
narrow apertures

the temperature
of select frequencies
begins to rise

what fluid sloshes
in the basin?
quicksilver?
or dioxin?

a seizure is
not a dance
the acrylic
nightmare pulses

what is troubled sleep?
staircases abound
mostly cracked and ruined
faux marble looks promising
but crumbles under
the lightest step

are the properties of
matter truly fixed?

08.13

austere mountain paths
with limited color palette
harsh geometries and
a dearth of winter fruit
ensure sparsely
populated walkways

in the foothills dread vines
entwine the feet of
timid walkers

with a hipflask and a flute
the fearless walker ascends

08.14

the nocturne lulls yet
the sun still shines

sensitive ears long for
the comfort of woodwinds

the earth opens up
fetid black water
gurgles to the surface

a single sustained note
gradually awakens a listener
to the dangers of
the growing swamp
whose smell is now
enveloping everything

the colors are changing now
or maybe it's the
quality of the light
greenish streaks can just be
made out on the
ruins of temples
—faded verdigris—

paintings used to line the walls
of many of these blue-
green churches
every martyrdom was made
bold and bright by the
toxic beauty of heavy metals

08.15

eternal bird creature gliding
high in rarefied air
sees false patterns in
circles and squares of
unnatural green surfeit

unnatural colors of man
bleed into the earth
in the interstices bloated
conurbations groan

dead-eyed citizens calculate
ratios against thermodynamic
stupor

potent spells and
urgent chants
are shadowed now in
mathematical dirges

modern alchemists oversee
a vast hoard of pyrite

black energies build in the
refuse piles to the
east of the city

and to the west dark songs
issue from the necropolis

warning against life's
pointless expansion

right angles collapse under the
weight of their sullen
contradictions

the bird creature glides
indifferently
toward the last
remaining forest
where the dead wood is
transformed into dark glass

08.16

do sinister forces
manipulate these atoms?
lest these effects are generated
by random collisions

each rotation has a
color and a shape
location and velocity
only apply
in this flat black dimension

white blurs smell
like death and
a smear of symbols
communicates
nothing

08.17

colors expand and
cosmic radiation
contains some unknown

concentric circles are
superimposed on pavement

a walker opens herself
up to impossibility
and feels electricity
crackle within
her moving limbs

and soon the limbs
of dormant trees
will draw on
subterranean energies

will birth pangs accompany
the arrival of new colors?

08.18

receptive faculties drown
in colored data and
high-pitched tones

the light's angularity
is changing

every shifting pattern is a
ladder of crumbling stone

some inclines appear infinite
every ounce of mass is excess

08.19

appropriate motion
or forced locomotion?
transit of shapes in gray
—bleak conveyance—

each walk seems to be uphill
the repetition of familiar
images is a form of blindness

some bland urgency drives
bodies across the plain

many forces hold
objects down
dreams narrated in
middle-european accents
wind down

where is the color?
how will it be transported?
the paralysis of grayscale
dreams is temporary

08.20

expectation mingles
with dread
at every set of gates
psychic enclosure
generates strange wave forms

guarded perimeters aren't
worth transcending—
urgency again
and a certain thirst

the streams of exquisite
inebriation will not be
found at this low elevation

inside the gates of the city
sober-souled citizens swill
the brackish waters
of stupefaction

08.21

somewhere a secret form
whose shape cannot be known
and atavistic sounds from
instruments made of stone

—not much to go on—

a pattern of sound will
guide my motion
models of many structures
rotate in the air

hypothetical constructs yet
a faint hiss and the scent
of acetylene suggest
substance somewhere

has this sense data seeped
in from some other
dimension?

lush correlations unfold

08.22

metallic planes bend
and vibrate
sending out waves
some sounds recall
the paralysis of
unlimited options

a faint ionic charge
has travelled a great distance
or none at all
to fill my head
with its pure minerality

some structures cannot be
kept beneath the surface

through the opacity
of the morning air
new shapes emerge
ubiquity of faint energies
suggest this is a cusp

there is an infinitely
small point where
two worlds touch

08.23

cardinal points are
hopelessly confused
orientation shifts through
chaotic rotation

the filmstrip rolls
beneath our feet

forgotten voices
haunted us
but in the haunting
was a beauty

voices from another
dimension returned to us
the music's pull
is effortless

walking north without
realizing—heading
toward the purification
of one northern voice
we end up in the east

if a flute sounds
the cherry will blossom

08.24

change is in the air
positive and negative
charges clash

sound of war chant
and rain dance—
the atmosphere's
relentless warriors
shall be lean
and angular

the oblique
masses below
unwitting beneficiaries
of harsh vectors
and the failure of
balance to hold landscapes
in fixed attitudes

08.25

what motion will be perfected?
repetition is insanity
and repeated denial
is a subset of
imperfect percussion

the language of infants
contains all sounds
and communicates little
the noise of maturity
contains fewer sounds
and conveys less

some accumulation of layers
will reach the triggering point

pure movement commences

08.26

listen to discordant silence
nothingness jangles
the world is bloated
with a gassy void

mouths gape in quiet
rictuses of despair
swimming in static
trying to achieve
some shift in altitude

reaching inside for feeling
a voice will say
'adjust the vertical hold'

all stale images roll
before my eyes
in a loop
i pray is not
infinite

08.27

sterile landscape—
clean arteries transporting
interlocking zeroes

nothing is completely flat
what curve is perfect?

efficient transport

let a = nowhere
let b = nothing

motion is a fiction

dark hues just beyond
the periphery of
natural vision
gradually seep in

09.01

not transformation
but magnification

this is how it begins

discrete objects
pulse with energy

words from some
forgotten language
penned by a shaky hand
words impossible
to decipher now

some employ
amulets
hexes

talismans
attempts to ward off an evil

insulation against
external forces
lest they be magnified by
engines of iteration

09.02

somewhere in the middle
thick voices begin to chant
then higher voices as
we skirt the perimeter

voices repeat key words
with great urgency but
i do not speak the language

in the distance an old
androgyne hobbles on

the frayed thread of
these voices tethering
the creature to
some center point

does this tiresias
understand the words?

and when the thread breaks
will s/he utter a cry
or a barely audible sigh?

09.03

the seductive doom of
eastern voices—
misleading unplaceable voices
confusing rhythms abound

these sounds did not come
from some eastern periphery

voices emanated from the
silence at the very center

those not preoccupied with
questions of the
voices' provenance
begin to dance

in gray hillside towns
bits of color appear
a blue of blinding intensity
begins to crackle
with electricity

the winds pick up and
strings continue to vibrate
each string a different color

they send waves to
the north and the east

09.04

incessant percussion
of industry
creates a wall of noise
what is inside and
what is outside?
what could such terms mean?

all around paces quicken
eschatological cymbal clashes
put moving figures
in a frenzy

'now is the time'
they shout
but what is now?
what is time?

09.05

some walker laments
porting needless objects
and the manufactured need

she would consign a lifetime's
memorization of useless
data to oblivion

there was no use
and what is use?

this walking is the
willed forgetting

09.06

a cold burst of color
purifies the vision
or restores it

there will be three things
one will be a color
one will be a sound

these are two things
but there will be three

09.07

these systems of measurement
are imperfect
revisited distances telescope
beyond any known
vanishing point

the narrow back passages
it is said
preserve sanity
but black-clad acolytes
block the paths
they are pulling wagons
laden with the produce
of the city of man

where?
to what end?
someone clutches a vial
that might contain a potion
with potent mystical
properties
or a highly concentrated
poison

at some boundary or limit
faces are scarred by
hunger and confusion

scars are hieroglyphs
or maps of other eras

as internal pressures mount
a wide path opens but
beyond some horizon
a crowded wicket awaits

09.08

ancient prohibitions are
no longer spoken
but their unspoken
proscriptions
remain in place

ungoverned motion
leaves tracks that form
metaphysical arabesques

if each step is associated with
a musical note and
a specific hue
what then?

music and movement
are not predictable
laws are not immutable
they strangle a single
moment in time and space

the ancient city
returns in flashes
its lawgivers and
men of science
have perished

09.09

right angles slumber
the theorems and proofs
have collapsed

curves and irregular
wave forms dance
through the warm air

patterns are shifting
the ears of fear hear
ominous sounds

but these tones alone
cannot be said to mean
one thing or another

the muted landscape
always harbors some
chromatic mystery—

waiting not to be solved
but discovered
and savored

09.10

these are rising tones and
they compress energy
into a sphere

only by pushing
away this nexus
of cruel forces can the
illusion of time be dissipated

on the outskirts
matter is attenuated
anyone who has ever walked
or anyone who ever will
can at these moments
walk amongst us

there will be no
tramping of heavy boots

under clear night skies
footsteps light and sure
are only just audible

footprints are left
under the stars
but they will wear away

09.11

dark siblings blow shadows
strange vibrations send out
shoots of new life

there is an old manse
set back from the path
there a curator of
secret frequencies
hoards and protects
eccentric wave forms

such sounds
may induce
syncope
vertigo

hysteria

strange reversals
are not uncommon
but the sounds
of affirmation
are bestial grunts

09.12

the temple bells have rusted
their oxidized chime
a dull memento mori
for any walkers who
pass the abandoned monastery

higher up a bright
periodic chime
marks time for
those who
attempt to climb

many sounds repeat
but these identical
tones are somehow
each different

just as the meaning
of each proffered word
is changed as
the word is heard

09.13

who is speaking
unpronounceable names
amidst this din?

discordant horns
and thumping drums
drawn out high voices

all is gray rain
and the broken
remnants of civilization

percussive interrogation
but no answers
are forthcoming

sounds of excavation
become audible as if
some mystery
might be unearthed

one patient crow
sits atop a mound
of fresh dirt

in this fractured
landscape it waits

09.14

an imperfect copy
lurches and lumbers

inferior rearrangement
of molecules is
a mockery of man

replication has
continued apace

only copies now
propel themselves
across the surface

their trails form
patterns of deception

outside so-called
habitable zones does
the primal force lie dormant?

09.15

the colored harps
have come unstrung
fragmented voices lament

fugitive glissandi still spark
the clocks are turning
backwards
and the masses descend
gleefully into a second
childhood

mournful strings
tell lullabies
and small gray eyes
search for bits of color

09.16

gradually energy is restored
or redistributed
spins and counterspins
had slowed almost
to a halt

for a brief moment
everything comes together
and the flutes sound

some new dance
sends rays of color
into the atmosphere

this is vision
this is a vision

movement smooth and sure—
inertia's chosen dervishes
push the energy

spectrum of sound and music
defies reason's cold prism

the walls are leaning

there is beauty in
the black flower
a pure trance awaits

the walls will fall

energy was confined
to information banks

now it explodes
in all directions at once

09.17

disembodied prayers collide
expectation has been
hollowed out
and its empty shell will
collapse in on itself

some green expanse has faded

many have grown accustomed
to the deafening noise of man
if subtle sounds should beckon
they will not hear

blunted senses and
bloated bellies
they go in circles on all fours
carrion lines the path
but carried by the wind
is a single flute note

09.18

these lamentations
mark the vision
that was taken from them

fixed sightless eyes and
the polyphony of despair

voices join together in
a rising hum
a buzzing hum
the sound of a swarm—
premonition of
some new tragedy

now the air starts to grow thin
though our altitude
remains unchanged

insistent cawing
of yesterday's crows
only now computes

09.19

glass strings bring
frictionless textures

this is a web
for navigation
not predation

some will wander
fractal pathways
where new
frequencies combine
and hearing
is perfected

09.20

muffled voices announce
the great malfunction

periodic chord progressions
up and down
back and forth

translation of color
fails again
each color freezes
at a different temperature

empty symbols could be
invested with new meaning
each molecular combination
could be renamed

eventually pointless crescendos
fade to static

09.21

baroque arabesques
of sonic textures
complexity builds on itself but
within the fine meshwork

the same old symbols
are hidden
green forces penetrate
the random sequence

the tapestry of the senses
has two sides
the weft flows under
and over the warp

on the other side of
the faded image is
its brilliant reverse
seen only by
the cool stone of
some ancient wall

the warp remains
unseen
unheard

unknown

09.22

predictable rhythms
drive the city dweller
through her perfunctory
movements
she is robbed of energy
by gray shapes
and given to believe
the small circles
she keeps making
constitute success

she is an energy source—
nothing more
when she is spent
the gray shapes
will move on to other hosts
leaving behind an
empty carapace
imperceptibly merging
with the pavement

09.23

the second cycle is prohibited
guardians of mysterious
mineshafts
discourage excavation
but the mysterious particles
escaped from the veins of
dark ore long ago

the mysteries guarded through
well-robed priestcraft
are hollow
dead-eyed cantors offer
impotent incantations

elsewhere one who
wasn't seeking
will find a transparent sphere
just visible against the
colorless winter sky

and now a beautiful chaos
of eastern vibrations
along with the divine aroma
of garlic and chilies

the old priests fast in silence
while we let out a woop
and begin to feast

09.24

did some warped power of
invention come into play?
similar voices tell
tales of distraction

voices waver and
try to break out
of the pattern

these are not new sounds
and we are right to
dismiss them

09.25

pools of black ice
reflect silence
in back alleys we dart
from rhombic shadow
to rhombic shadow

one man from the dream
must be avoided
the other one sought

interlocking shapes pave
the surface of nothing

09.26

a poisoned dream
falls into place
the nausea of low frequencies
reorders various shapes

bassos and sopranos
alternate distorted
benedictions
but the voice of the enemy
will freeze memory

new light floods a
narrow passageway
there are many white doors
to the left and to the right
all are closed and locked

the sound of darkness grows
as the passage narrows

mute remnants beckon

09.27

at the edges lies
the myth of permanence
heavy breathing
fades to silence

madness is
momentary revelation
sanity is
a lifetime's distortion

beneath the
sounds of the ordinary
is the wisdom
of a toy piano

the same pattern
that lulls
can awaken

solitary moments
shape the movement

compressed gasses
form evanescent
messages
then disperse

10.01

some warning siren
breaks through
dulcet older tones

piles of dead matter
support some
spotty growth

soon a ceremony
will begin but
many paths are blocked

a fixed sense
of orientation
is laughable

those hands
frozen in prayer
may no longer
grasp or proffer

malformed arthritic joints
posit topographies
of mute despair

what intuition
lies beyond
pleasing frequencies?

and where are
the three geese
flying?

they slice the white sky
obliquely keeping
for the moment silent

10.02

insectile revelations
strangely beautiful

the butterfly's voice
is surprisingly
resonant
and melancholy

bells toll as i await
a message of sadness

the subtle voices of
the others come together—
an urgent warning
i cannot fathom

the vegetation is sparse
the voices are fading

oxygen feeds sinister ovens
and the madmen gibber
lost in these echolalias
i wander dazed

10.03

profound sense of depth
vitiated by discernable
middle range waves

unreliable sense
data recedes

the void is only
ever skirted
to plunge in is
to make it
disappear

between two binaries
lies an answer
that is not an answer
to a question
no one thought to ask

the repetition
of two colors
bodes ill

a wild crocus opens
in the cool spring air
and a wooden flute
longs to sound

high and tenuous
it will begin
then a playful trill

walking nowhere and
looking for nothing
i find it

10.04

sonic confusion as
the great distraction
continues

farrago of notes and chords
to overload the senses—
more useless data
feeding misleading
calculations

some snap fingers
some stamp feet

a thick white foam
froths at the mouths
of the believers

in a dark shack
outside of town
the apostates
empty bottles
and make music

10.05

one mournful element
accelerates its complaints

its chaotic particles
spend fierce energies

other elements will
reabsorb these energies

the color of movement
is mysterious

shifting hues feed
on energy exchange

and resist the dull
monochrome of balance

10.06

these waters do not heal
incredulous souls are
dunked in toxic fonts

clever distortion will
relay coded messages

strange juxtapositions
will continue apace

cold metallic droplets
rain down upon all

we wait for a moment
in bleak vestibules
waiting for the elements
to realign themselves

dwarfs with whiskbrooms
shoo us away and
we return to
the heavy onslaught

cold and relentless
a rain of nails continues
and i look down at my hands

quicksilver stigmata

10.07

rapid recombinations
send out vibrations
the organic and
inorganic merge

bearded ones
send messages through
unlikely couriers
and still the mallets tap

the phrases
shift and merge
rhythm explodes
triggering ancient memory

many spheres are
set into motion by
celestial percussion

10.08

wordless muttering and
unsettling vibrations

the path north
is incremental
and the height of
myriad peaks
varies greatly

a new language is required
one suited to higher elevations

they may be placing
newly risen loaves
in stone ovens

we will be drawn north by
the smell of baking
and the sound of
new words

musical words
magical words

10.09

the voices of desire
are insistent
but these
engines of avarice
are silenced
by a plucked string
from the near east

the humors are volatile
and lie in uneasy balance

red smears
suggest caution

vanity exercises
its sagging belly
as bits of twine
and faded paper
blow slowly to
the northwest

10.10

no light no shadow
a body at rest
under a parallelogram

thick fluid
fills a chamber

the concepts of
interiority and
exteriority are
no longer valid

low notes and
phantom drones

absolute immobility
does not exist
somewhere a hand
traces small neat letters
that spell out words

to ask what the words mean
is pointless
time make the shapes
because it must

the chamber empties

a soft light suffuses
the gray of
the endless sky

10.11

distorted reflections
in old mirrors
accidentally
convey truth

high notes
and
low notes
collide
leaving
sonic shards

faint shades color
the edges of perception

in cool air
plucked strings
trace warm messages

10.12

the same words
keep returning
each time
they return
they lose
their force

words that
dissolve into
pattern regain
their power

pure vibration
penetrates surely

the perceived world
breaks down
into shape
color
sound

components can be
reassembled and
rearranged

every atom is available
and these atoms can be
subdivided by the subtle mind

surface and substance shift
bringing the birth of
new words and new worlds

10.13

a faint residuum clings
to the vast surface of time

impossible measurements
and a booming voice
barring thought

the native perfection
of our inner voices
replaced by alien words

10.14

without warning
voices cry out
in treacherous melody
nostalgic recollection
fades to stupor

but were these memories
placed here by
malign forces?

the gray fiction
is penetrated
here and there
as red and blue
rays intersect
forming a delicate
structure in
the middle distance

its reality is ephemeral
but a figure can be seen
climbing it and moving on
to some other realm

10.15

sound of friction and
constant movement of objects

structure built for an
unknown purpose
the spin of anger's electrons
wants to be reversed

most of the heretics
have been carbonized

the wind still blows
carrying voices
lifted in song

10.16

colors and textures recur
merging as sounds merge
moving through this
many-hued sonic texture

my pace quickens

one by one each
extraneous voice
will be stripped away
until all that remains
is the pure music of

silence

10.17

numbers repeat in patterns
too complex to be grasped
by the limited minds
of this plane

these are clues and
must be intuited

these ratios have penetrated us
voices will intone
a series of lists
familiar names
repeated quickly

do these slurred syllables
serve some purpose?

singing voices are transformed
into pure color
and every shade is distinct

each shade has a
corresponding number
strange calculations
could free or enslave

10.18

austere coincidence weaves
subtle threads into the pattern

ancient voices caress and
encircle modern technologies

mediation metallic
or magnetic or
both

images coalesce
for a moment
then dissolve

sacred perception transcends
the blunt efficiency
of the senses

10.19

forces of propulsion are not
subject to direct influences

the ground itself is shifting
yet its reality is a
matter for conjecture

structures are erected
and razed

concentration on a single color
or a single note can pierce
the sonic hues of
mute confusion

back through the
fiction of time
to the mystical
elongation of sound
and the ecstatic
collision between
presence and absence

10.20

a second string is plucked
two frequencies interweave
some periodicity holds
us in its thrall

unpredictable currents
drive groups of atoms
into different patterns

their traces are invisible
to some eyes—
inscrutable to those
who see without vision

trapped in a hostile valley
devices pump and churn
furiously

dynamos run full-tilt
misnamed power or energy—
what is it all for?

10.21

sound expands in
concentric circles
a pulse of bright light
infuses the texture
with abstract energies

duration and drone
as categories
and constraints
dissolved into
atoms forced
to recombine

a series of long-held
tones suspend me above
the terrestrial surface

every curve and every angle
can now be seen as
pure form

10.22

electricity resonates deeply
leaving tracks

the electrons of disaffection
hum and buzz

soothing voices intone
what might be
the final lullaby
just above a mass of
discordant sounds

brown anticipation
seizes the unwary

energy gathers at key points
these concentrations are
available to those who sense
their presence

10.23

a familiar sound
coming from the
opposite direction

the tree bark looks
like brushed metal
some sounds grow
more mechanical

geometry's duplicity
camouflages a
small stone structure

strange new tones
emanate from the structure

metal crickets
chirp electrons

loose molecules vacillate
between polished surfaces

temporary songs recall
the old elements and
call for their return

their power—mighty
because indiscernible—
will wear away

10.24

every one of
the new elements

until clear water flows
over glass-smooth stone

movement begins and
duration would seem to be
inversely proportional to
acceleration or have we
been trapped once again
in rationality's sticky web?

find beneath the rapid
alteration of notes a
nearly inaudible drone

many will march to a beat
wearing confused smiles

on another temporal plane
all is perpetual drift

10.25

gelatinous smear of words
forms an endless pavement

a great sickness might
bring one low
confusion reigns until
the ill one finds a way
to see through to
the other side

let the voices intone
untranslatable words

let shapes change color
and tones rise and fall

10.26

two waves composed of
profane morphemes

no one chants them

small humanoid forms
scamper up trees

from this high vantage
the fissures in the wall
become apparent

new names and
unpredictable angles

there was once a sacred drone
and an unknown
tree in bloom

now chance plies the loom
and lets madmen
find meaning where they may

10.27

there are limits
harsh codas

what though is the
nature of a limit?

there is movement and
the passage of time
or the appearance of such

could some energy escape
these metaphysical confines?

particles projected
could reassemble and change
the nature of things

11.01

movement is slow

stride compressed

progress incremental

pain and sorrow constrict
the taut spring at
motion's fixed center

there is a certain
hypersensitivity to color
but soon a degree of
liberation through elongation

11.02

expectation and fulfillment
are mutually exclusive

some await the
bright kingdom
some live in thatched huts

points form lines
lines form planes
planes form solids

progress's sure enclosure
masquerades as teleology

electronic chimes vibrate
and generate the perverted
energy that would bind
each individual point together

walking through a
wall of noise
one moving particle
longs for stillness
and silence

11.03

mallet blows precipitate
fractal explosions of color
but behind that shifting layer
is a heavy sea of gray

the bifurcation of thought
pits mystic vision against
cheap fantasies of banality

at the furthest reaches of
dynamic equipoise
lies madness

two spheres exert
variable forces
upon one another

the crystalline sphere
calls for perfected vision

but the leaden sphere's
dense powers are
all but irresistible

who would sing a
song of gravity?

who would float
effortlessly?

11.04

one primary color dominates
not monochromatically
but in sporadic bursts

known forms unravel
strands composed of
highly charged particles

workmen attempt to
reassemble them

there are two interlocking
patterns but the workmen
can only see one at a time

11.05

suddenly bifurcation
seems ubiquitous
and secondary
colors explode
tinting the
intersecting lines
as well as the
parallel ones

11.06

it starts with a door
the name is misleading
thoughts are not movements
though both can be wrong

the walker keeps moving

when he strips away
his name he will
step out of time

11.07

balance disfigured
then rejected

wordless voices chant
what might be warnings

hollow forms
dot the landscape

a rapid repeating pattern
encloses some and
they are lulled to sleep
by the sun's
indifferent warmth

some merge with the pattern
and a few of these
break free from
its centripetal force

they float above a long path
from this vantage
they see it ends
in a cul de sac

broken pencils
litter the path
loose paving stones
shift erratically

11.08

the floating ones
utter syllables stretched
to such length as
to have become

pure sound

perception shifts again
sometimes back to
an unmistakable
chord progression

then a burst of
powerful electronic sounds
serenity and rage
unravel the delicate linings

all communication now
the manufacture of
distracting noise

within this sonic chaos
is one pure note

11.09

damaged souls revel
in their own din
drowning out with
their colorless noise
the blue red black
white yellow
of the pure
la so mi re do

11.10

three elements suppressed
and a single note
keeps repeating

something is stirring
acceleration through oxygen

unwelcome notes seep in
at the edges

be on guard—this is not
the time for forward
movement

not yet

11.11

one future day is posited
myriad voices intone its name
and cry out for unknown
geometric forms
imbued with new colors

repeated words will
always lose their meaning

one word over and over
soon pure sound
then vibration
motion
then rest

and silence
again

11.12

a time was confused for a place
expectation and silent waiting
is not rewarded
nor is the arrival

the movement is the place

when a walker stops
a mystical city dissolves

11.13

interlocking shapes are
densely packed
within the walls
somewhere in the distance
forms perfect themselves

in open space
forms merge their
differing voices
and project them through
the air's tenuous medium

each note is charged by
collision with
ambient particles
some listen but few hear

a single flute note
will generate new structures
and destroy the ones
crowded like stones in a wall

11.14

industry expands its
pointless manufacture of noise

each fragment of
sound attempts
to crush the crystalline sphere

the surface is infinitely pocked
and chipped yet no fissure
threatens this passive orb

clear voices are raised but
the din of dystopian
equipment
is nigh absolute

industry apes creation
its finite structures are
pure illusion

all this interference is
the collision of sounds
from two different worlds

11.15

there is a corrupt heart that
takes rest in the
coarse weave of
a pattern whose
intersecting lines
obscure a narrow pathway

lightness and darkness
together
create this shadow path
blue companions will hover
near the edges

the moment of rest
becomes never-ending
but the walk goes on

11.16

categories collapse
in upon themselves
strange instruments
reshape the
structure of space

random interpretations
of irregularity
will hold meaning if
one seeks it

vague constructions
are part of the additive art
but who shaves away
superfluous matter?

11.17

one night in spring
jupiter appeared as
three arced bands
with a hollow center

this was a circle
broken in three places—
each equidistant
from the other

observers cried out
'what can this mean?'

and i heard a voice
and the voice said
'black water'
and the rains came

what is tritium and
what is deuterium?
what is plutonium?

traces of dense silvery terror
can always be augmented by
dark ingenuity

the voices said
'what white fire
could nullify
this water?'

11.18

dense lacunae

forces press in
from all sides
compressing
this void but
intensifying the
potency of
its energies

a walker may
access these energies
she may pass
through the void
absorbing energies
and transforming them
into pure color and
shifting shapes

particles and waves
might pierce the
opalescent skin of
this infinite emptiness
made small

they too will be transformed
nothing may pass through
without being altered—
a part of itself absorbed and
purified by the emptiness

11.19

the sound of flux
rejects fixed forms
and dead ends

words produce words
whose patterns are
ever shifting

dull minds cannot
fathom our mystic
consubstantiality
with the elements

this is the sound of
everything merging

11.20

textures disturbed by
an elemental imbalance

once again the ink runs

could these letters be
frozen into some
semblance of meaning?

slow motion smears and
smudges mock by
almost meaning

droplets of liquid
adhere to almost
every surface and
things have slowed
almost to a halt

scan the horizons
for incremental movement
for some sign of life

11.21

why count and catalog
fragments?
haughty voices cannot sing

the true pattern is subtle
and never the same twice

taxonomies and accumulations
of data are illusions

each utterance is broken down
further and further into the
quarks and leptons
of apparent meaning

still the energy of the ineffable
suffuses all horizons with
unknown colors

11.22

a new sound is learned
unseen gasses take on
greater significance

liquids and solids are
momentarily held
in abeyance
by the mind's lethargy

notes sound in triads
sounds grouped and repeated

warning caws pierce the air

the walker scans the skies
for a white crow

mystic gossip shakes
tree boughs
ad hoc congregations
are scattered
by fierce gusts of oxygen

this does not concern
the walker

11.23

contradiction recurs as
time burns itself up
warm sounds and
amphibious vision
alter the shape of space

sounds generate themselves
tempo and duration
do battle within
a many-sided shape
while a crow looks on
from far away

caws echo

11.24

this white-blue energy
burns coldly through
the atmosphere

all shapes liquefy and
flow formlessly
seeking new containers

the sharp pinpoint of
hyper-localized pain
wants to explode into
universal orgasm

11.25

even in the well-insulated
homes of non-walkers
the elemental clash
drums its punishing rhythm
upon calcified heads

implacable deluge swallows
all evidence of man's folly

the wind's ire blows across
sinister flutes while below
the earth waits impassively

above
warmth and light convalesce

11.26

rare glimpses of the south
many hues grow vibrant
the intensity of light
is dazzling

energy is transmuted
rhythmically
the warmth of repetition
imparts old wisdom

interlocking circles
appear everywhere

transformation fuses
old and new for
a split second
then destroys them both
beautifully

11.27

contradiction of the senses

sphere of burning plasma
heated the earth's sure vectors
and they pierced the naiad
who would sing songs of
the daughter of the sea
as fierce waves pounded
the shore relentlessly

warmth burns
oxygen buffets
hydration drowns
earth swallows

12.01

they appear—
keep reappearing
one two three
four

entwined in single purpose
or knotted in conflict

if two mysterious principles
mingle
can their essence sustain?

embrace—escape
recognize the power
human ambition is
microscopic

granular fantasy
may be blown aloft
washed to sea
merged with the earth
or fused into the hard glass of
energy's shadow self

12.02

attenuation of recent density
low frequencies pull
heavy particles
with them

everything becomes
unpredictable motion

the dance of bright particles
transfixes

no prediction
no control

new vibrations affect
the saturation of
each color

from black soil
a clear spring emerges

at certain moments
all forces are held in
dynamic balance

12.03

the false utopia is
accompanied by syrupy strains

perfectly uniform
physical shapes

are penetrated by the
faint scent of
semen and death

mechanical butterflies
are viewed
through rangefinders

all organic experiences
replaced by the recordings

tapes playbacks loops

beneath the surface
a powerful magnet
wants to be unearthed

12.04

linear color pierces
the dull monochrome
lines grow and intersect

simple patterns first
right angles and
safe perpendicularity

eight million lines intersect
and at each point
of intersection
new colors form
new voices speak

simple phrases first—
a new sound from the east
emerges and
sinuous waves form
expanding outwards

tempo increases and
heat vapor shimmers
across the skin of existence

electronic tones repeat
magnetic chimes draw us in

the collective mind wandered
perhaps tropical notes
conjured brown bodies
and the taste of salty skin
permeated the will's
indifferent talents

we had sheltered
for far too long
beneath the convenient
shadow of an overhang

everyone agreed the
jutting structure
had the shape of
enormous buttocks
and it blessed us with
a miasma of rectal cologne

percussion joins the
pattern of color
pulling us into the light

blind at first
our sight is incrementally
replaced by vision

12.05

movement to
movement fro
some transformation
begins its work

potent energy
takes many forms
though its force
can be sensed
its essence may
not be harnessed

submitting to it
fuses you to its
powers

pure propulsion
creates a trail of
transparent curves

12.06

flute notes woven into
the texture of space
call for ascent

beeps and bleeps
send coded messages

12.07

repeated phrases gain
mystical significance
even nonsense sounds
repeated over and over
create frenzy or stupor

heavy air contains
toxic droplets

one hand traces shapes
the other erases

this is the moment of
admixture

time's gossamer sash
has a small tear

someone collects the refuse
nothing is left

12.08

no names or titles

all spots on the map
mysteriously effaced

circular movements
and consumption
send out vibrations

susurration of a
gentle breeze
sustains a
fugue of birdsong

industry's din
wants to blot
all out

i let the wind's
song sustain me
as i walk and wait
for the sound of
a distant flute

12.09

profane image
blocks eye and
clouds mind

we move uncertainly
through signifiers
and symbols

a scrawny white man
with spectacles
wants to block the path
to the higher realm
he would take the
bread of truth
from our mouths
his insipid sound
lulls listeners
to the final sleep

move through colored shapes
and rhythmic wave forms

the white hairs of
base distortion transform
into the deadly shards of a
broken funhouse mirror

keep walking

12.10

a perfection of sonic textures
marks the speaking of stones
ludic sounds guide walkers
through the shifting landscape

but static and feedback
have their place

metallic linearity vibrates
into three dimensions
generating lush wave forms
as oxygen moves above
the surface of an iron sphere

never quite making contact

12.11

shifting ratios of movement

travel posits origins and
destinations but
purity colors the space
between the points

space infinitely divisible

upbeat tempos and
elongated strides
are meaningless

one plucked string
and one drumbeat
rectify time and space

12.12

a bright darkness begins
chromatic dynamism
gives the edges the appearance
of rapid movement

transformation must
become a state
not a condition
between states

could the evaporation
of gross physicality
be constant?

a note can only be
held for so long or
repeated so many times
before madness blossoms

what of its intensely
sweet fragrance?
prolonged dark sonorities
are accompanied by visions
of cathedrals in ruin
and the tears of
a beautiful woman

12.13

alternating charges
inhabit the spiraling
air currents

sounds and symbols
are used and misused

adepts learn words
one letter at a time

somewhere a magician
is groaning as a
stone pillar turns
itself inside out
forming a passage
deep inside the earth

words from east and west
collide and intertwine
forming a double
helix of sound

the calligrapher wants to
touch up the letters but
his fat hand wipes out
the answer to
a silent prayer

12.14

a brown voice from
the near east
slurs prayers against
dissolution
he has consumed the
harsh distillates of truth

simple repetition through
a dry mouth

a certain cup contains
fire water earth air

drink deep and
exhale blue dreams

clouded mind and
sore muscles
seek clarity and relief

information explodes
geometrically

the dream voice cannot speak

12.15

questions of sources
and origins
form strange vectors in
empty space

unknown textures blanket
the surface
heavy silver water pools and
boughs are laden with
toxic fruit

viral grooves infect the sinews
creating a peninsula of dance

lean bodies propelled
by chemicals
seek red energy

12.16

structural forms
created from the repetition of
western recapitulations

water wants to flow

signifiers melt and
opposite colors bleed
into one another

somewhere one posits
an instance where
motion is fiction

ideas are spotty like
fungi on a wet tree bough

resolution can't exist

12.17

a distortion of lines
creates strange frequencies

a long sequence of constants
communicates nothing

something automatic will have
a cumulative effect

serial or cyclical
repetition and pattern

the uninitiated scratch
their heads
and pound their fists

meaning leaks through
subterranean fissures

some random blot will restore
elemental outlines to
this molecular confusion

12.18

there is a fragile miscellany
in four parts
what part outlines
the properties of a sound?

and would its bardic creator
be able to unravel
the shadow and the man?

high notes come fast
digital and analog
bleed together

now low notes
succubi pluck strings
and imperfect heat
creates uneasy percussion

oversimplification and
a fear of synthetic colors
kept us from seeing that
oppositions weren't mere pairs

they sent vectors out
in every direction
and the multiple intersections
formed the fabric
of the universe

12.19

rest now but
no different from
movement

pointless conjunctions

forces in combat
within each atom

named binaries expose
cosmic impotence

all languages are dead

12.20

we think of eastern fluids
infinite varieties flow
with subtle distinctions

mystic distillates—
we drink
northern concoctions
and a sign appears
a number whose
meaning eludes us

inhale fire
exhale colored gasses
elemental conjunctions
are embodied in
fragile containers

postures prove
the vessels are empty

is every void's
existence tangible?

the most rudimentary
ladder leads
down as well as up

12.21

universal paraphrase
generates hollow chants
rough hollow skin develops
repelling particles of
unknown charge

surfaces are studied
and classified
the smell of rancid
fat is always
just beneath the surface

behind an invisible wall
plastic rats swim
in a chemical syrup

dark eyes set in hollow faces
long to see secrets
concealed in the ruins
of sacred structures

without thorazine
a black man prays

orderlies from the
nether regions
don the white gowns of
holy men

they are coming for us all

12.22

solids dance in the air and
a faint tingle activates
these containers

water flows and
awaits the grand distillation
it is what the spiritual
shall consume

12.23

explosion of blue noise and
shockwaves make
fissures in time's façade

deep low tones and
liquid spheres announce
obscure streets and
remote passageways

what did these
oxidized cylinders
carry away?
and did they
carry it away?

clap hands in
vague repetition
don the hat of
our ancestors
and cut through
the gray weeds

pavement shifts and
mud is slick

stone paths are littered
with metaphysical debris
a blue door and a white door
are stacked on the
rubbish pile—

portals to rare beauty
disguising themselves as trash

12.24

chromatic saturation
suffuses the borderland

tattooed homunculi
populate this liminal space

many moving figures
but most are not real

at the moment of transition
reality seeps through

at the core of each
animated shade
a small metallic sphere radiates
image streams

small signs exist—
talismans against
crossing over into madness

12.25

study without mastery—
they memorize arbitrary
names and enunciate
them emphatically

their silver disk is
scarred and cracked
life's dry remnants
will be reanimated
by an electric raga

suddenly some will dance
against the noise
of meaningless words

12.26

bright sun and
black sound fuse

lugubrious spores
spread in a fine dust

the magician sneezes
transforming the
air's indifferent
medium into an
infinite chamber
of trapped particles

every tone sends a
pulse of colored light

each hue changes the
medium in different ways

the marks of transformation
read like hieroglyphs

12.27

life's painful inversion
embeds us in ore
earth's ritual immersion
yields sterile symbols
colored around the
edges a faint orange

three witches concoct
strange potions whose
consumption unearths
a mineral egg and offers
a path to the woods of
the other whose air
tastes of blissful panic

oneiric dust induces in
most an ontological sneeze

translate the spasm of the real

13.01

golden cones betoken
dream readiness
signification shifts
every code key is outdated

silver grass has
an ammoniac tang

when the air has
the clarity of a diamond
breathe deeply

pools of black water are
rimmed with purple moss

low strings send
vibrating messages
as the androgynes wait
for the dance to begin

13.02

matter locked in
recurring patterns
keeps its own counsel
meaning is collapsed in
revelation's dream color

many are blind to these hues

a fading sound traces shapes
rotating lines limn
triangle and hexagram

curves elongate simple shapes
and make new forms—
they pulse with blue light

13.03

pinpoints of bright
evidence mark
an explosion across the sky

the concrete wilderness awaits
attrition's inexorable
wrecking ball

stale matter will cry out
for transfiguration

humanity dedicates itself to
the manufacture of excrement

notes sounded on a flute
have no mass and
the doors of
abandoned abodes
create a simple shelter
decorated with colored air
and perfumed with new wine

13.04

etched lines record the vision

movement through
light and shadows
ruptures this demi-reality

are lines of escape marked
over or under the surface?

vagrants climb
invisible ropes—
insects on the strings
of a tiny violin—
making notes
accompanying their
pointless back and
forth motions

13.05

clean tones emerge
from the east
pure sound calms
cellular ruckus
and discourages the appalling
mass of excess

repeated tones and
economy of motion

a temporary pattern structures
our composite particles so
now distractions from
oblique angles are
reflected away
into the ambient chaos

13.06

a third coast opens up
in the middle of dry land

percussion of chthonic mallets
mingles elemental forces

the earth's dull monarchy
gives way to an anarchy
of brilliant light and water

both contain charged particles
whose energies pulse
through bathers' bodies

electric skin and
shifting curves
meld into a new landscape
where all the senses are
merged into one super faculty

rows and columns collapse
into a single cell

the hammer blow of
instantaneous knowledge falls

13.07

bundles of light create
sounds of strange intensity

pulses of dense energy
punch holes in the veil
of separation between
two worlds

for a moment matter
is malleable again

forces of compression
and geometrical constraints
are in play in the
worlds on either side

in between
something is happening

13.08

floating in the earth's
diseased embryo
the illusionary ground shifts
but we walk

the molars of false reality
grind truth into a fine dust
and the digestive juices of
rationality transform beauty
into clear odorless excrement

13.09

extinguished fires blossom
from decorticated stalks

the snails of divine madness
define genius

small bent trees
invent new colors

the straight lines
have all receded

the infinitude of points
describing that vanished line
have dissolved into a
nothingness of pure electricity

a palsied quadruped
attends an ancient woman
who stares off into space
dreaming of colors in
black and white

13.10

blinding yellow light
steals oxygen
and the faint crackle
of electricity
is never far away

hide in fragrant shade and
count each fragment of stone

silver threads crisscross
with otherwise
worthless bodies
forming more networks—
pathways for energies
unknown

silver spheres orbit each other
a certain frequency will
alter their course
changing the color
of everything

13.11

strumming like mystics from
worlds old or in between

incantatory chords fade
giving way to smooth
repetition
then incremental adjustments

ephemeral patterns shift
through sound and space

two wizened sentinels
guard a red brick line
barking sharp warnings
in a highly inflected dialect

machine tones now—
clean and pure—
marking precise intervals

now the walker's medium
is unadulterated oxygen

his imperfect body shares
the rarefied air with
remarkable sounds and
perhaps new colors

13.12

a faint hum expands
announcing numbered secrets
they will be filed away
with the others

empty compartments are
stacked near the edge of town

abandoned shells haunted one
walker who entered the
penumbral alley
seeking light

there a box once used
for conjuring
was smashed upon
the pavement

a color that was no color
gained a profound saturation

one note expands until
it fills the cosmos

13.13

anthropomorphic forces
shape these curves and
define these limits

strange sounds and
blue stones
but familiar too
that tone and that color

a graffito of thwarted
desire bleeds from
a crumbling wall

voices taint the pure sound—
a moment of experience
replaced by the mendacious
promise of meaning

13.14

time's plastic telescope opens

a robot dirge mourns
oxidized metals
silicon melts
in white flames

in the midst of the
charred ruins of
structures housing machines
is a pool of pellucid water

13.15

dormant awareness
rises to the surface

technocrats attempt
to create water
in arid labs
their white coats a
flaccid mockery of
secret egyptian rituals

counterfeit forces rule
wherever the true
energies have fled

lean rag-clad magicians
hide in plain sight
they know the
secrets of transformation

13.16

sounds of tunneling
or perhaps building—
an escape vehicle?

look—
all the colors have
changed slightly

centers of gravity
have shifted—
new ratios apply
and no rapid calculations
can approximate them

urgent sounds structure
molecular formations

lithe limbs move surely
though the path
be ever-shifting

once the limit is breached
it is no longer a limit

13.17

manufactured insects
burrow in deep

coded messages could
identify the portal

but in this forest of
decomposing fragments

all language
becomes tangled

all is reduced to
sound and shape

13.18

constant flow—
repetition cannot exist
every time a word is
uttered its meaning changes

rivers flow altering
the shape of the land
golden flesh glows
under the sun's insistent rays

waves and particles
in constant motion
a body at rest is one
temporary rearrangement
of atoms

it will change
and bodies in motion
create chance patterns—
contrapuntal ink stains at
points of intersection

13.19

obvious interpretation
of a song
choreographs a clumsy dance

wait

sounds must penetrate
then spread through
every muscle

it's not the meaning
of repeated
sounds but the meaning of
the repetition itself

incremental changes work
within each auditor

every motion will
be smooth and sure

colors change as bright light
darkens some things
and lightens others

13.20

smooth surface breaks
into uneven segments

here and there
the skin peals away
revealing fine
metal wires

an ad hoc man
shambles believing
for a moment
that he is real

even he knows
tropical flowers
sometimes bloom in
northern latitudes

13.21

vibrations trace the
shifting surfaces
of new solids

slow movement
through muted colors

simultaneous touch of
warm and cool makes the
surface of the skin electric

transmissions from
somewhere far off

these pulses were
transmitted eons ago
only now are sensitive
bodies feeling their presence

13.22

description
analysis
exegesis

a confusion of
distracting noise
bleated out by rationality's
priest caste—
their iron robes
pin them to the surface

painful linear progression
but gravity prevents them
from understanding
the curvature of a sphere
or its ineffable harmonies

13.23

disturbance of thoughts
progresses apace

a familiar cycle of sounds
will draw you back
to a point

points become lines
lines become a plane
planes trace the surface
of a solid

13.24

what story is told
in an unknown language?

song of wide open spaces

there would be bright sun
and wide blue sky
but somewhere a
stone tunnel leading
into darkness

the underground flowers
bloom in muted tones
cool respite from the
painful blue of an
infinite sky

13.25

would we hear with kepler
the music of the spheres
if the myriad voices in
pointless yammering
could be silenced?

what is the color of
each sound?
and are these colors
fixed or shifting?

and even if the colors
themselves are fixed
the eyes are not

rod to cone
cone to rod

blue intensifying and
the discovery of
a new red now

what if these notes
functioned on a
cellular level
within each body?

to feel each sound
to be each sound

13.26

vibrating at
identical frequencies

attenuation
        dissipation

recombination

organic sounds come
from the north
what was called a diversion
was the calling

through submission
to external
forces comes power

wisdom-lined faces
from iceland
        from finland
                from norway

aquavit-clear eyes
portals to inner notes
sounds heard only once
but remembered always

13.27

elongation and color
saturation
bodies move as if
they were human

music in the middle
distance and
dark spheres orbiting

what might they portend?

return ticket and
dragonfly's faded body
pressed together
into the pavement

vision of the earth—
a scorched black ball

14.01

colliding surfaces generate
new but familiar frequencies

blades of metallic
blue-green grass
cover a raised mound of earth

a pattern of circles frames
a square opening

part of a stone wall
is peeled away—
it was only the faintest façade

colored cylinders dot
the landscape
as a profusion of weeds chokes
out everything else

automatic lamentations
strangle
the vocal chords

14.02

translucent blue-green stones
are found at intervals
along the straight road

some will stop and gape
wondering at their meaning

one improvement
after another
led to a spasm of destruction

the pavement is grooved by
heavy machines in preparation
for more improvements

the vines are heavy with
flavorless fruit and the
straight road is a
noisy drag race

the slate gray clouds are heavy
and time rides a blue bicycle

copper nails will crucify
another oxidized saint

but somewhere beyond a
dense thicket of
confusing data
lies a crooked path

unused if not useless path
unseen if not invisible path

it lies beneath a
favorable constellation

14.03

seemingly incompatible
sound waves flow
together

the resulting notes
are green but
tinged about the
edges with red

industry tries to
drown out these
new sounds
with brown noise

what would ancient
voices say?

would they
have seen
this sound?

could their
rudimentary
rods and cones
discern the color
of the shapes?

might they summon
in their defense
a pythagorean
chord sequence
tracing the lines
of a golden rectangle?

14.04

a sharp whistle as
time folds in upon itself

linear progression is
an origami crane
sitting on a shelf

a bell rings

two crows watch
from a copper gutter

memory's edited filmstrip
runs in a stale loop

the bars of a wrought-iron
fence enclose but
the shadow of those bars
on the pavement forms
a ladder leading to eternity

14.05

contrapuntal currents
shift perception rapidly
back and forth between
two points of the compass

tempos outpace
analog human potentials

it's not disorientation but
freedom from the
constraints of space

thought passes
from shape to shape
taking on the form
of each new vessel
and filling it

expanding and contracting

light once fading
burns strongly now
but only at the edges

where it meets darkness
there is a soft glow

is it the medium for
some new organism?

14.06

drumbeats and rapid
woodwinds
sketch a martial scene

an old crone has stolen
the fountain
and walled in its waters

minor chords bubble
beneath the surface
and the crone gossips
about thirst

men and women march
around the perimeter
whistling through
chapped lips

sporadic figures in the distance
mount a hill

confusing sounds
midway between
east and west fade

suddenly the sound
of a stream
and a flute drunk on
choice distillates

14.07

fast now
short sounds
and rapid movement

earthy drumbeat
counterbalanced by
ethereal tinkling of bells

many count the spheres and
each one comes up
with a different sum

blocks of wood clap together
and metal threads vibrate

coughs expel pneumatic
fragments
and the leaden body
sinks again

bodies flock
schools are formed
techniques of mass
production refined

concentrate on one note
and conserve breath

layers begin to peel away

14.08

something was not
as it seemed
anticipated gain
concealed within
a great loss

a cobalt blue hum
scrambled a cosmic egg

voices made a new sound
and scholars constructed
lexicon and glossary

no one knew that
the voices themselves
were the language

the words the scholars
thought they heard
were just noise

14.09

the sound of moving air
collides with the
vibration of solids

bombardment in
slow motion as
grass turns red

a bird perched
on a silver disk
makes no sound

silence like cellophane
wraps the forest
but within these
woods an old style
of making sound revives
sending waves out
in visible rings

the trees in the woods
grow at odd angles
and etched into the
surface of the soil
are what could be
symbols or
random patterns

14.10

known boundaries dissipate
in the face of absolute
movement
with shifting identity

fixed attributes reveal
themselves
to be a reactionary fiction

stable meaning is
still cherished
by some skeletons but their
monochrome doxology is toxic

now drum machines
tape loops

mixing boards
and the sound of
violet light exploding

14.11

this is the relative north
the atomic weight of oxygen
remains unchanged

rod and cone here too
register the shifting hue
of blue's expansive
bandwidth—
compressed wavelength
with near infinite potential
for communication

the names of streets
are dream-familiar
light burns through
the dirty panes of
an abandoned structure

transparent brutalism—
the archaic and the
hypermodern sit
in quiet juxtaposition

hieroglyphs mark
back alleys and
splashes of unexpected
color create a map

useful markers as
streets shift their
orientation imperceptibly

14.12

like some daredevil
bursting through
a paper hoop
i break through
to the other
side of the map

printed names
faintly visible
though meanings
are reversed
when read
backwards

strange creatures
populate these
busy streets

three letters
repeated and
an insistent drum

trees sprout
from cement strips
and metallic vines
encircle their
submissive trunks

voices are speaking
an unknown language
that sounds something
like the color white

14.13

light and dark stripe
the pavement
black squirrels are
strange attractors
whose psychotic movements
trace unknown shapes

three peaks each marked
by a secret sign

a certain frequency
and a certain color
will mark each path of ascent
some follow the shifting shade
some scramble over
bright metallic scree

what eyes see that under the
depiction of the three peaks
is an arrow pointing
downward?

14.14

blue and green cubes
float in the middle distance
they lack solidity yet seem
fragrant with substance

though formed from straight
lines and right angles
they represent
something round

the outside surface is
mapped imperfectly
onto the inside surface

sporadic wrinkles occur
between the two surfaces

14.15

a sign has been torn down but
residual adhesive
traces patterns

sections of pavement
receive colorful images

a neo-haruspex interprets
strange coded messages—

reading the stone and metal
interstices of an
eviscerated city

14.16

sudden shift in the air
rotates all visible
objects a few degrees

tones deepen as
ad hoc sculptures
dot the landscape

residue of a civilization
what of its mystery objects?
empty space between them
offers clues

14.17

yet further north
as myth has it
location of
exaggerated
gravitational pull

what sounds emanate?
not flute notes

there moth wings
would be crushed to
the ore-laden earth

beware sudden
increases in mass

to continue the ascent
we must now descend

14.18

motion beckons and
alternating notes
create a cadence

the air's fine texture
wants change
alteration charges
these stray particles

a crystalline dome
traces its structure
in the colorless air
as rhizomes force
subterranean maps
through dense soil

14.19

beginnings and endings
duration
wet study in dry heat

familiar voices will
form themselves out of
any raw material at hand

intensity varies and
data shuffles itself
between the
apparatuses of sense

flashing light or
choking perfume
is a single data point—

there is suspicion that
all data has undergone
some fundamental
manipulation—

its inherent duality
flattened out and
translated into
arabic numerals

denotation
          specificity
                    rationality

a series of shapes
traced in the air

14.20

accumulation and
expansion form
a serial pattern

sound waves expand
into a cone of warning
or a call to prayer

full containers
surrender
their utility

empty vessels are
transparent so
cannot be seen

can the beetle's
malachite shell
be questioned?

14.21

vectors of force
suddenly shift and
direction changes

colorless movement into
a field of simple sounds

vibrations resonate
tempos accelerate

short wavelengths
dominate perception

curves and intricate
spirals are suddenly
visible amidst
the gray
rectilinearity

air feels depleted—
breathe the bits
of color left
in the atmosphere

feel carefully
for the fulcrum
on which is
balanced the
visible world

14.22

staggering movements
create dissonant sounds
confusion seeps
into everything

asymmetrical shapes
flash upon the
shifting colors
of the sky

uneven pressures
act everywhere

there are some
who are acted upon
like particles
in a chamber

black roots put
sonic tendrils
through a landscape
whose outermost layer
has been peeled away
revealing something raw

14.23

reassuring sounds as
the water rises
then periodic
repetition

music becomes the sound
of a clock running down
the clock's supposed
progress is binary—

tick-tock
on-off
zero-one
black-white
life-death

does time erode the edges?
or start at the center
and work its way out?

what is duration?

during this speculation
the water has risen
above our heads

perhaps too late
a warning voice
can be heard

but in this dense
medium words
cannot be discerned

only a lush drone

14.24

premonitory crackling became
a series of identifiable notes

senses sharpened by
the meddling left brain
but once i (or someone else)
listened
there was nothing
worth hearing

unworn hat slid to the floor
its floppy brim recalled objects
half of which were linear
the other half curved

part of a formula was
scratched on the ground
and crumbs of food
were disdained by stone birds

playful sounds nullify
the senses

compass points spin
wildly back and forth

14.25

glass structures erected
structural complexity
perfect transparency

language whose
sound and meaning
are the same

impossible language

words
compressed
elongated

sounds manipulated
sampled-looped-remixed

could language be
translated into
pulses of light or energy?

14.26

there is rapid transit
there is metallic enclosure

this is not one of those things

hollow tubes serve
many purposes
shallow thuds construct
a rhythm
pattern empties the mind
distraction dissolves

two men board the same train
same time
train speeds nowhere
underground

two men are shadows
built from
gray at the edges of
random letters
and space between
repeated half-notes

14.27

strands come together
imperceptibly
in the sprawling pattern

every note has its counterpart
two parts of the sound too
perfect to hear
the notes cancel one
another out
and lull us into
contrapuntal dream

all data passes through
the mind-fugue's
psychedelic processor
notes chromatically
broken down
by sound prisms into
pixels of color
arranging and rearranging
themselves
in infinite patterns
waiting
to achieve
silence

15.01

higher faculty
links disparate elements
or intimates
supra-rational connections

the clean tone of a single bell
constructs an entire universe
and brings it to ruin

dream world came first
this world formed
from its desiccated droppings
and the spittle of
a mid-level god

15.02

false confidence in
names and naming

smug manipulations
of information shift units
according to pre-
ordained rules

insipid soundtrack
at high volume

but under certain
circumstances
sound bends
this is atomic swerve
this is metaphysical drift

categorical stench is
reabsorbed by heavy metals

transformation is nameless

15.03

nocturnal percussion
gives way to
vast electronic pastoral

digital ruminants consume
charged particles and
process them
voiding data

piles of fresh steaming data
dot the metallic grassland

collection and distribution
spread this byproduct
throughout the conurbations

it is the unit of exchange and
the building block of the
newest megalopolis

15.04

evidence and
counterevidence—
really just a false pattern

time and color are disproven
under a nonexistent sky

the vapor of experimental
language
disperses their remains

synthetic colors
recalibrate vision

linearity will give way to
bends-shifts-swerves

15.05

bitter herbs spread
emitting silver light

underground roots
act as portals to
another dimension

music pulses and flows
viscous colorless liquid
absorbs and reflects
oscillating cyclically

sound grows metallic
but not rigid

waves collide
forming the curves
of a silver sphere
attracting sound and
containing it until
silence returns

15.06

no name—
just as well

naming = control
control = illusion of control

not all movement
is governed by
external forces

when the flute sounds
titles of things
will be stripped away

each note is spontaneous

somewhere down below
a man measures
the length of strings
calculating tones
and harmonics
while the lips on the flute
taste of new wine

15.07

adjust the volume
knob dial button
adjust the contours of sound

sound has a shape
if not many
plucked strings
and bowed strings
draw different lines

variations occur—
perhaps nine

shifting textures and
no identifiable speaker

to take in at once
the parts and the whole
requires bicameral truce

15.08

are differences in
scale significant?
what is decay?
what is half-life?

resonant concepts elude us
sometimes there is a speaker
sometimes there is a reader
for a moment they
become one
then dissolve

is all communication just a
residue?

15.09

expectation of vertical lines
rising and/or falling
in parallel
gray silver white

metallic lines make
unexpected sounds
'why no something new?'
a voice complains
yes
but did the old somehow
contain the new?

did the linear streak of silver
create the ambient
sound waves?

suddenly spheres
are misshapen
there is a flattening

invisible forces act
what is a silver sound?
and merged with
gray and white
in parallel
what chord will sound?

15.10

molecular migration
animated like some
electro-static puppet

particles ricochet
with plastic pings
there is randomness

pure periodicity
would of course end in
amplitude death

follow the links
but there are none
follow the links
because there are none

building drones merge
a ting of metal on metal

strings vibrate at
certain frequencies
uncertain frequencies

in dreams the metal had a
just perceptible curve
and the curve
or the metal
or both
created color—
blue and green
perhaps yellow

15.11

muted horns and
refracted light
the sounds of words but not
their meanings
velocity without motion
parallel rows of
imperfect spheres
suggest a forgotten function
or formula
or equation

a series of intersecting lines
triggers cognitive
compartmentalization
shuffle and reshuffle data
to reassemble
balkanized geometries

15.12

manic affect driven by
northern voices
repetition held sway
for a while but
reversal is an option

contradiction in every
sense is applicable
contra = against
diction = speech
or the opposite
or the other side of language

only ever have one
side at a time
language against itself
its phantom self

how proceed?
what structure for hanging?
look for meaning where none?

com-mu-ni-ca-tion
break|down

15.13

book of sounds
book of words
two different things[?]
same[?]

there is the shape of letters
combination and permutation
there is the shape
of the mouth
position of lips tongue teeth

there is the voiced
and the unvoiced

there is vibration
sound waves travel

fixed meaning explodes

just particles
then propagation

each sound becomes a smell
word inhalation
infection

syntax?
diction??

15.14

scrap of paper with letters
between sender and receiver
message failed

students of residues
reassemble scraps
they posit intention
impose meaning
where there can be none

everywhere fragments
if seek then find

an old symbol
with other trash
two parallel suns
have burned away
its red blue yellow

just a faded outline
remains

15.15

not much to work with
never is

where the words fail
revert to
shape color sound

dream language is
immune to translation

shapes shift

no pure colors
only the space
where they bleed
into one another

and beyond the edges that
were never there

15.16

compressible sphere and
flat metallic disk

pattern dictates some
movement
the old patterns of shape
and sound have worn thin

sharp smell as disparate
compounds are mixed

motion must push beyond
even the seeming futility
of a circular movement
tracing ever-widening
representations of these
new axes of rotation

moving always further
from the center
but linked to it by
imaginary radii

15.17

asphalt voices and
a dark room filled
with prepared pianos

someone is calculating
instantaneous rates of change

a dead hand is frozen
in benediction

heavy voices like solid objects
immovable voices drain color

a dead hand is frozen
in malediction

echoes of electric psalms fade
the air still heavy
with metal ions

15.18

words and numbers
vie for supremacy
but even words and numbers
only add up to
a clapper-less bell
an empty alembic

watch the strokes as
each figure is limned
in india ink
in the motion is the sound
in each shape is the substance

15.19

green smells permeate the air
the light from
acoustic lanterns
cannot be harnessed
or directed

its wave-particles are immune
to digital splicing

sound and light move
in the same medium

there is ambient electricity—
galvanic dream energy
draws messages from
metal ores buried
deep beneath the earth

blue sound returns
it is cool and round

15.20

chaotic transposition of letters
words change shape
and meaning

syntactical rupture

brief explosion in the
cerebral cortex
unleashes meaning's
harsh asymptote

15.21

intense heat and burning light
of pure energy is unendurable
translation into
knowable forms
furnishes the penumbral void
with hollow objects

does a transparent spherical
membrane contain nothing
or give shape to pure oxygen?

15.22

stippled ellipsoids in
an in-between space
no x and y axes could measure
their interiors

derivatives and integrals leave
their dimensions unknown

they expand and contract
making subtle music

15.23

east and west cancel
each other out

the large sub-humans
are watching
they drink pure metal
and exhale compost piles

these neck-less enforcers
measure dimensions and
take color samples

shapes must be regular
hues from an approved palette

one cranks a device
that sends out widening
spirals of noise

if signals are sent
noise spirals will
cancel them out

the large ones mostly
guard against the
return of silence

15.24

back and forth
through doorways

objects cycle
from opacity to
transparency and back

ignorance builds upon
itself until it seems
like wisdom

structures made of stone
and the erosion of time
form a blue cube

mournful sounds elevate
till stones weep tears of joy

15.25

organs groan
their deep sounds
struggle to rise
into the atmosphere
but gravity pins them
to the earth

notes from plucked strings
twine and intertwine
around the trunks of trees

high voices eschew reality
in favor of the fantastic

somewhere someone reads
the dull heavy thoughts of
scholastics theologians
philosophers

no surely not

letters and numbers in light
flash auguries of consumption

factories transmit
smoke signals
to one another

industry echoes the
dead sound
of history's mute organ grinder

15.26

clean high tones purify
a northern voice
always returns
ancient language whose
words have lost their meaning

communication through
blue vibration
the portal is not
where you look

pure sound
pure voice
pure velocity

the secret urgency of stones

letters and trigonometric
forms mark the pavement

insistent humming
peels the paint from
outmoded structures

15.27

periphrastic messages bounce
chaotically between
six green surfaces

they lose mass with
each collision

structure and repetition
or the appearance of such
or the desire for it

easy solutions
offer themselves

wait to hear two flutes
in counterpoint
they shape a finite pattern

sounds bouncing around
in a colored cube

gradually
winding down
like automata

16.01

elongated orbs pulse
with potential

after gestation
trapped energy departs
music so quiet compared
to machinery

though what if a
machine music
could drive spirals through
the tight design of
right angles?

rings of energy float
above geometrical remnants

16.02

sound travels up like heat
cognitive walls have
become metallic curves

a new movement begins
familiar but unnamable

how many sides does
a heroic shape have?

or do its curves map onto
several dimensions at once?
rendering the concept
'side' archaic

in and out of structures
rituals are taking place

some shapes cannot
be stopped
because they are
not yet known
they will change as soon as
knowledge of their
forms is approached

16.03

remnants of corrugated iron
at the heart of the rubble

oxidized rebar betrays
the ghost of structure

sounds of jaunty locomotion
come from no clear source

the light from a nearly
burnt-out sun or perhaps
several lesser moons
puts a silver filter between
apocalypse and its
hypothesized observer

the beauty of wordless voices
in an un-peopled landscape

decay's aesthetic perfection
rusts the gears of
intricate clocks

sound waves still travel
though here there are
no men and there are
no hats

ruins wane and saplings wax—
iron-age fairy tales

16.04

movement is slow
biding geological time
until the paltry evidence
of humanity is eradicated

this is a time and
this is a place
just not
this time
this place

liquids scarcely flow
appearing as dense
clear solids
sound is tactile
natural objects
emit tones and
vibrations

this is the
sentience
of stones

the aggregate grain
of human achievement
is lost in the desert's
laughing infinity

16.05

impermanence and
uncertainty
masked by a numbered
sequence

action and contemplation
are two things

the same tone is repeated
clean and metallic

sonic hypnosis and
natural movement

planes and curves and
patches of color

the circulation
of particles

no grids no lines no arrows
motion dictates its own shape

janus faces east to pray
and west to die

movement's secret drift
points north for the moment

16.06

state and phase change
no beginnings or endings
black transition and
the moment black and
white become one

this could be a path
(the space in between)
the sound of bells
periodic rising and
falling of notes

movement guided by vision
rather than sight

new intensity of color
moisture weighing
down the air
but paralysis as
a northern voice
contradicts itself

some fruit
never ripens

16.07

small sounds grouped carefully
give rise to a voice's nebula—
eerie beauty and
instantaneous communication

when a wordless voice sings
voice is pure language
words are another language
together they cancel
each other out

parallel lines appear to ascend
one voice like the wind
at high altitude

shifting frequencies and
the emerald belly of a beetle
devoured by other bugs

trees have rained seeds down
upon the pavement where
they cannot take root
or only over long
periods of time
at great effort

16.08

archaic horn blasts
from another hemisphere

drones in the flood plain

plastic film unspools endlessly
and three voices
with heavy accents

voices with the texture
of rose petals

time-bound letters and
numbers as the sky darkens

colored spheres bobble
incongruously in grey sky
heavy with metallic rain

green curves and the
superimposition of structures

microscopic tones cut
fractal patterns from
an unknown material

16.09

counting and clapping
are suspect
structured movement and
predictable expectations

bleached foliage accompanies
old tapes played at half-speed
control mechanisms
undercut the automatic

open to computer-
generated sounds
open to random
open to pattern
mix it all together

or watch it as it shapes
its own shifting contours

drift with them

16.10

separation of different worlds
by a thin membrane

in each world the properties
of green things vary

the blue sounds of
mallets on a hemisphere
generate awareness

here are desiccated things
organic and inorganic
fragments

voices lull and awaken
somewhere in between
they send a message

the homunculus stays
in the trunk
bodies moving freely
have no fixed dimensions

16.11

mud songs and a
confusion of categories

a horseman drowns in
liquid pampas

liquid thick and
silvery like mercury

debris explodes
across the sky

everywhere the
smell of burning plastic

some humans will
sprout a new set of limbs

and learn that happiness
is a series of automated tones

the calliope slows and its tones
at reduced tempo
sound sinister

humans scurry on
all sixes looking
for fresh water amongst
this sea of stones

16.12

acoustic laments in the
shadow of a large insect
(perhaps mythic destroyer
of crops or messenger
from some other place)

scored lines and
ambiguous words
mark a series of circles— flat
two-dimensional disks—how
could such messages
have substance?

vibrations of two
frequencies intertwine
premonitory sounds
and a vision of birds
—dark and metallic—
the sound of their
unreal cries etches
lines in stone

16.13

strange mathematics as things
don't add up as predicted
known formulae must have
missing elements

impassive stones
here and there
reabsorb shifting
molecules of iron
voices implore—they purport
to come from another
dimension

voices promise utopia
they are the ghosts
of technicians
they witnessed the
white-hot explosion

they engendered the
great bifurcation

16.14

perhaps one note
sent into the atmosphere

it engenders other sounds
sounds make new shapes
and from these shapes
temporary structures
might be constructed

16.15

decaying royalty mourn the
passing of their realm with
lugubrious dances

the sky is clear
strings are plucked first
then bowed

now clean air
and bright light
but muted colors and
a vague blur around the edges

question returns:
is this a duplicate planet?

something is off just slightly
color shape scale?

copy of a copy

incongruous yellow door
portal to where?

16.16

two automatic processes
occur simultaneously
one is creative
one is destructive

what results from
their combination?
a dance on shifting
currents of air

crimson sounds had
warned us but by
the time we heeded the
warning the sounds
had blackened

third eye is put out by
millennia of low-
hanging branches

there is always a
layer in between
making contact only
ever approximate

voices come from tall grass
they sing of supernovas

16.17

heavy smell of coal tar
but just beyond the miasma
the surprise of cool air
and dense foliage

blue-green spheres
and a ziggurat

old sounds
infuse the ground
and carve a series
of gentle undulations

violet messages
erupt from the sward

a series of points that
might be joined together
might in fact be linked in
near-infinite configurations

bones litter the roadway
perhaps the remains of
those lost in patterns

16.18

dense expressions in
counterpoint
communication
resists translation
and the mendacity
of paraphrase

east and west are woven
so tightly together that
each one ceases to exist

shifting correspondences—
color tone letter
number shape direction—
spark moments of recognition

in the central plain
saturnine sounds

green things sprout
from cracks in the pavement
plucked strings mark
a different time
and under concrete's gray—
black soil

16.19

pale voice blue voice
translation into units of sound
new apparatus captures signals
pulls in all ambient
transmissions

how to sort all this data?

is this dissonant jumble of
tones a warning or a clue?

disorientation again—
vaguely dystopian sounds
but oddly beautiful

this is a different voice
drifting locomotion as
the music pulls us
in a widening spiral

16.20

this is some kind of after

ominous sound of toy pianos
a ring of black soil and
wood chips waits silently
to punish whoever
laid the sycamore low

in the distance
the sound of his saw
is just discernable
crows circle
with fixed radius

the woodsman takes
the trees one by one
and one by one he
expunges words
from the lexicon

a voice intones names
one after another
or maybe the same
name repeated

impossible to make it out

16.21

zeros and ones hoarded
malleable ciphers
sometimes money
sometimes data

tall structures were erected
mercantile temples
a choir of pinstriped eunuchs
intone sacred numbers

zero zero one
one zero one
one one zero
one one one
one one one

until the walls collapse
and the numbers are
submerged within
static's frenzied dance

16.22

what is a song? what is voice?
what processes enfold
sounds into the texture?

beneath the image
silver threads
trace an outline—perhaps
a shape like a face

someone has remixed the
sounds of machinery

metallic receptacles
collect voices
process them
loop them
transmit them
as breath

respiration in color
sonic hypnosis and
a series of questions
            suppositions
                        subjunctives

once a human voice sounded
like a train whistle heard
only by a white dog
whose spasms of
mute howling
gradually
subsided

16.23

chromatic diversion

these metallic streaks
have specific colors and
represent speeds impossible
to calculate or comprehend

a self-regulating sonic force
drives mass forward

sudden changes in direction
—reversals even—
are not uncommon

a fine mesh expands
until its silver web
covers every surface

time now reveals
itself as a blue curve

16.24

blinding solitude edits
its own finite glossary
these symbols have
beautiful shapes though
they mean nothing

one inverted letter is
made strange and new
and what of a long
curved blade emitting
repeated cycles of notes?

someone would name this
then the music would stop

distant signal fading out
looking for solace in
nameless static

16.25

drawn back through
layers of distraction and
bogus interpretation

wading through white fluids

underneath this noise
was a single flute

the only liquid was wine

white—almost clear—
tinged with silver

we drink pale moonlight
exhaling across a flute

is there a way to become
a shape a sound a color?
refined to purity of expression

doing nothing

not rejecting exertion
because to reject is to exert
not to speak because
to speak is to lie

we don't have a name
for this thing and

16.26

to name it would
do it violence

we cannot know it
can only be it

line with an arrow on each end
opposite forces but
are they equal?

these are diminishing forces
and they act on everything

movement slowed by
a pervasive heaviness

there is nitrogen
there is oxygen
there is argon
there is carbon dioxide

a jaunty hissing then
the realization that
there is not one frontier
not two but three

the air itself was obscure
now one kind of vision returns

16.27

one line extends from
a central point
movement seems free
tracing an arc in either
direction but
always at a fixed distance
from the center

notes recur in a minor key
two white squares share a side
as if waiting for more
to tile themselves into place

equilateral with fixed
dimensions

the curves chords and arcs of
tethered motion can be
combined with the
changing sides of
the growing rectilinear
structure
creating a map of these sounds

17.01

factories churning out
transparent objects
they might have sounds
trapped within them

sudden drop in temperature
and surfaces crack
names spill out accompanied
by notes in a minor key

information explodes
across the sky

the foremen at the factory
bark out orders—
information must be
collected and maintained

but the workers have disrobed
and fled into unmapped streets

transparent fragments
reassemble themselves
into new shapes

now they contain
cool air and silver light

17.02

change crackles in the air

voices were raised to
a visible shape but
what if a shape should
violate the laws of space?

would ancient hymns
be silenced?

polyphonic chant
gives way to a
sequence of beats

the timelines have
invisible points
of intersection

a northern voice
resurrects an
ancient epitaph

there are strings and
there are pipes
but underneath
a computer-generated drone

17.03

visible undulating wave
traveling east to west
then back

from another perspective
it looks like a spiral of
highly charged particles

a strip of juxtaposed images
runs in a loop faster and
faster until friction burns
a hole in the film

black dot with bright corona
spreading outward until the
image is annihilated

finally something worth seeing

the impermanence of curves
smells vaguely of
cleaning compounds
surfaces will be spotless
scrubbed to nonexistence

perfection

17.04

hammers strike bells
brown smells cloud thought
everywhere electrons
are being exchanged

calculations of rates
and distances fail
a colorless circumference
shifts position but
casts no shadow

movement is slow and
traces a small circle
or perhaps an ellipse

the suggestion of edges
or limits though unspoken
is ever present

bright light reflects off
a flat surface offering
a possible model

17.05

no fixed signifiers
there is a reflection
within each reflection

this is a toy infinity
another distraction
while faint lines and
curves trace uccello's
chalice in the sky

the volume is
always changing—
measurements
are pointless

movement is jerky now
with a tape loop of
pizzicato strings
and non-metallic
percussion

break out or
break through—
the accompanying
sound will be
glass shattering

17.06

signal and noise—
the fast space in between

completely novel information
inscribed on a cicada's
spent container

voice lifted in song
the sound of some
ancient language

do discernible stimuli
fit within an established
structure?
shifting sense data
will alter its shape

the repetition of
unexpected sounds
has rendered their
sonic outlines
familiar

colors washed out now and
faint smell of rotting
vegetation

clocks are winding down

old machines whose purpose
has been forgotten
dot the landscape

mounds of newly
excavated earth
encircle the remains
of what was
a convenience store—
a cromlech for late capitalism

17.07

intertwining spirals of ascent
are mapped onto
three-dimensional space

form was thought to
contain within it
meaningful content

there are sounds
whose timbre
has no earthly counterpart

one rare color
pierces the monochrome

sudden marks left quickly
on the pavement no longer
convey any message
if they ever did

litter increases rapidly now
as the worn pavement
descends

there are some who would
read messages in this rubbish

its shifting meaning unfolds
in its textures and patterns
of decay—strange beauty

17.08

certain qualities are
defined by their absence
cool air and limited
range of colors
unseen chemical reactions
alter the landscape

strange voices breathe
ionic canticles
impossible to discern
any meaning
posit an underlying system
performance mustn't
undermine competence

subterranean associations rise
this is upward motion but
is arrested half a meter
above the earth's surface

what fire prevents
further elevation?
and what of the rapid
duplication of the color white?

17.09

not strange sounds
just more of the same
but new fruits are
ripening on metallic vines

gray dominates this
temporary landscape
there are no shadows in
the gray-land for
the land itself is shadow

metal trees shed oxidized limbs
concave disks are mounted to
the shells of former habitations
in stillness they wait to receive
signals that never come

17.10

layers combine in
interlocking patterns
a sonic field suggesting
perhaps
the final movement

strange instruments
from another time
create sounds with
more dimensions
than we thought existed

one plucked string
sends out a vibration
that ripples through
filtered light
and managed color

somehow this vibration starts
to change everything

what is frequency?
how many herz?

indefinite cycles within
its own malleable time

17.11

synthetic life forms move
chaotically against
this poorly painted backdrop

just past the blurred edges
lie the structures of
the hyper-real

flat planes and curved surfaces
become one

the great migration begins

the sound is of the stochastic
bouncing of a metal ball
as it makes its endless descent

one voice cries out:
'who among us is real?'

in answer comes the sound of
a great machine laughing

17.12

the cusp of transformation

hypothesize: humanity
is a construct
produced by a random
configuration
of information

postulate: reconfiguration—
end of humanity?
posthumanity?

everything is after
within the confines
of linear time

could this be a
digital dirge?

atoms of red and
atoms of blue
undergo superimposition

there is no such thing as
a single color and
light will not be mastered

the data is shifting

17.13

telescoping sounds throb
and reverberate in
contrasting colors

there is singularity
there is negation

there is a convenient
construct—
an approximation
that allows us
to make meaningless
calculations

what is underneath
melodic skin?
atoms divided

the color of the surface
is slowly bleached away

a phantom blade spins
across the sky
erasing words
in reverse

17.14

polished metal passageway
frictionless curved surfaces
reflect and distort

the wind has blown green
clusters of oak leaves
to the ground

in the distance a bluish
dolmen mutely embodies
impossible communication

ores were scooped from
deep beneath the earth as
lightening turned
sand into glass

the high-rise harbors
ancient forces in its
skin and skeleton

in the morning the high-rise
consumes the energies of
those who enter

in the evening the high-rise
expels their spent shells

17.15

many forces acting in concert
could they be unraveled
into distinct vectors?

objects are acted upon as
flower petals deliquesce
on concrete

solitude is not a cold land
though it sometimes obtains
in the far north

the pattern is shifting
former knowledge disordered
former structures
disaggregated

the sounds of time
seem stationary
but recordings can be sped up
or slowed down until

past and future
oscillate
in opposite directions

17.16

the ire of inanimate objects
generates unnamed sounds

high notes from
another latitude
pierce blue skin

once inside these sounds
metamorphose and spread

in some the sounds
engender change

for others altered
sonic particles
attack healthy cells

those who survive
experience slow
movement in
strange media

time as the illusion
of movement
through laminated layers is
one explanation

decomposition leaves
black streaks
where words once were

17.17

how to measure the angles
of an abstraction?
how many degrees describe
the span of the indefinite?

strange reversals produce
unknown fruit

a perfectly preserved body
is posed on the pavement

piercing adjacent layers
manufactures time

lost in the sound of
synchronized mallets
striking surfaces

and the beeps and buzzes
of electrical current
carrying messages invisibly

this information abides only in
straight lines and right angles

in known and unknown
languages a madman
speaks of money

his incantations rise and
collide with power lines
momentarily revealing
information's false idols

17.18

compounds are
combined in solution
potion or poison?
someone will drink it

supposing transformation
such an imbiber
might become
sound or color or shape

if shape then compression
first lines within a flat plane
regardless of number of sides

all those lines fold in
on themselves
the resulting line
recedes from both
ends toward the
motionless center

the point shrinks
growing denser
as its circumference
grows smaller
function defined as a
limit approaching zero

never reaching it

17.19

sound of metallic carnival
rusted barkers lure fresh flesh

extracting and consuming
their energy
resets half-life clocks

it feels like the last days

childlike voices weave lies
into a sonic shroud

here and there the shadow
of a figure fleeing the funhouse

escaping from the carnival's
imagined perimeter

outside of these self-
imposed confines
lies an infinity of other zones

smell of old engine oil and
cheap cologne gives way to

garlic frying and juniper-
infused spirits

17.20

a fading whistle left
a cloying taste
data shifts itself among
four quadrants
at a moment when
one quadrant
contains the most data

it tries to expand
eliminating the other
three quadrants
changing data and
shifting power
mark the euclidean landscape

heated particles are
moving quickly
within a cylindrical enclosure
their collisions transfer energy
one measures and records data

17.21

arrangement of voices
creates structure

strange metamorphosis

then persistent vibrations
invisible waves and troughs
slice and re-slice the
atmosphere
into new shapes

below the ground is
marked by parallel lines

is there something between?
does it take a shape?

the temples are empty now
but madmen gather near
their crumbling structures

wordless voices howl

17.22

thundering percussion brings
visions of pure metal

magnetic forces—
heat by induction—

many devices are
propelled at high speed

what of these crows
repeatedly scattered
from the pavement by
geometrical combinations
of ores?

real or robotic?

precise beaks pull
filings from oxidized
carrion sculptures

once thought imperishable
the surfaces are now degrading

one atomic combination
among many decelerates

17.23

numbered pieces
labeled parts—
assembly seems
a feasible goal

totality's illusion
is fragmented by a
series of discordant tones

structured movement
sculpts the contours of time
measurement continues
information increases

colors separate
and desaturate

interlocking grids
have been
rotated by degrees

rusted iron gates
protect faded paints

history's urgent message
is a faded smear

17.24

bilateral mantra pings
back and forth
percussion and vibration
generate random colors

some system of codes
yields finite combinations
some would say 'is walking
even possible?' all motion
being strictly circumscribed

identity is defined
movement is identification
space-time conflation

random objects are being
inserted within the grid
altering points of intersection

17.25

from ancient trance
to silicon sura
voices cry out in
linguistic patchwork
time's dimensions
stutter and shift

halcyon babylon
time's impetuous children
long to feed their
father hot stones

mottled curves appear
as north and south collide
particles explode everywhere

there is convergence
there is transmission

17.26

two black sounds intertwining
auditory fragments?

what is real
cannot be answered
cannot be known

posit: space as construct
further posit: time as function
of subjective perception of
shifting layers

consider a cracked sphere
consider its range of
possible meanings
from cosmic egg to
immanent system failure

a stringed instrument
either not yet invented or
impossibly ancient
creates apocalyptic tones

all will be black
all will be chaos

it could be an ending
or a beginning

17.27

if frenetic vibrations
are subterranean
will their energies
penetrate the root
structures of this
visible terrain?

latent visions are activated
letters and numbers
randomly combined
into hexadecimal incantations
to some electronic god

there are shifting
patterns in the sky
some see beautiful chaos
others a terrifying order

18.01

movement through
distraction and
misinformation

is there escape from
the guardians of data
and their control apparatus?

they've grown fat and
their power only
functions at nodal points

lean bodies escape through
gaps between these points

here unstructured thought
communicates through color

non-uniform shapes
curl and shift
this is a study in
blue green silver

the guardians
misunderstood
number

lean figures trace shapes
some magic must exist
in between

18.02

modular patterns can
only be discerned
one section at a time

an invisible grid
lays atop
everything

even the sky—
not just stars but
the space between them

observers of each
limited celestial field
stand on the red soil below
peering through instruments

a figure wanders off
dropping his instrument
but not the bottle he carries

picking up the broken
instrument
he shakes glass fragments from
a useless tube while scanning
the sky with naked eyes

he places the tube to
his lips and blows

bright light and pure distance
become modulating sound

18.03

first muted horns
from the north
then the growing of
a nameless drone

motion changes quickly

these objects resist collision
or are these subjects
said recently to have
disappeared?

desire reveals itself as
a pure metal construct
whose parts move
independently

dark heavy air now
slows motion

there is a transparent
curvature

walls are growing taller but
there may be a hidden passage

or perhaps expansion implies
attenuation then rupture

18.04

tape loop is running backward
heavy heat is not rising
sudden percussion atomizes
the immediate surroundings
into fine particles

do meaningful micro-
frequencies
exist beneath the
banality of chatter?

divide sounds and
rearrange fragments
structures must be
lean and angular

who intones the names
of catastrophes?

shifting drifting
repetition and subtle change

un-crush the pigments and
breathe form into
dimension's flattened shell

18.05

procession at double speed
the dignitaries now seem
laughable spastics

an oblate scrap of metallic
foil is the last of its kind

does the alternation of
two numbers imply the
necessity of choice?

not every code will
be broken—
cracked open—this is
the brute violence of meaning

small trees trace a line
not saplings but
ancient dwarves

their compact limbs capture
the scream of silence

enigmatic woman weaves
another world out of
unnatural frequencies

18.06

one world stretched beyond
semantic recognition

sound itself

uttered sound repeated
shapes something
beyond meaning

one voice rises
above the grinding
of machinery
inventing
new languages

the landscape:
shards of glass
abandoned structures
overwhelmed
by their own shadows
discarded packages
bearing names that
no longer signify

now the ting of
metal on metal
now the clack of
bamboo colliding

it is a fading song
but in the distance
what might be a lantern

18.07

moving toward oblique dialog
between prerecorded sounds

in some places contours
will overlap rupturing
the autonomy of shapes

drones and rumbling
reshape visible space

the blue sound of
a bell inaugurated new
angles of inclination

searching for one spot—
a pivot point where
reorientation
crackles and spreads looking
like an electron tree

some grime is trapped
between parallel lines
and the side where colors
fade rotates away

18.08

from a compact cloud
of dense smoke
voices and the eerie blast
of mutant trumpets

metal grates protect
openings to nowhere
knobs switches dials—
what do they adjust?

fine scrapings of
lead rain down
through gray-damp air

an old door with the
number 10 painted on it
or is it one-zero?

on the street a color
vacuum obtains
sounds are muted

artificial light creates
an argon nimbus—
a signal to visitors from afar

18.09

new tones at unknown
altitudes
down below darkness unfolds
dynamics and duration and
the possibility that the black
silence is not the interval
between the notes but the
infinite background
upon which
the notes are but
sporadic specks

and are the words
just back strokes
trying in vain to cover
a white void
when movement
ceases and you are
lost without recognizable
landmarks?

18.10

fast notes attempt to
chromatize the dull sky
there were repeated
announcements

many energies
become traffic
the noise of
success is deafening

on the outskirts
a lone flute
celebrates failure

the conurbation's
dense surfeit is no
match for a simple broth

the train tracks suddenly
end but for miles they
have been overgrown with
weeds and wild grape vines

hobos perch on
decaying ties
they sip new wine
under a half moon

18.11

the structure of knowledge
is a dark reflection that
artificial light can only obscure
while robot shadows
place numbers in a grid

adepts feel the changing
texture of the air
the ringing of a bell
creates a new source of light
and subtle sounds from a
muted horn spread
a yellow glow

sharpness at the edges working
inward then ripples
and shimmers
as the blunt senses
register information

the smell of garlic frying gives
evidence of intelligent life

18.12

time's red deacon
operates an orrery
little slipper-shod
feet pedal wildly
shifting the position
and relation of
these eight spheres

he huffs and puffs
at the center
like a dying star
poised for supernova

arteriosclerotic star—
will the spheres slow
then stop? or will
the deacon be replaced
by some young athlete?
and what color will he be?

18.13

unlikely conjunctions
create heat
sustained vibrations
and intermittent
chimes mark two
different kinds of time

they intertwine

the outlines of this
shifting perimeter
can never be known
with certainty

an invisible virus
transmits itself
through unwitting carriers
perhaps sound
perhaps words
perhaps strokes

the air is hot and cool
causing the skin to prickle

the machines too
feel the change—
within their vast
code a single mark
waits to inaugurate
the madness of machines

18.14

impossible concepts transmit
themselves through
strange sounds
shapes are changing and the
message's dense pattern shifts

there are objects in motion
and objects at rest
the color of each object
creates a string of notes
shape color sound

only temporary triads
no fixed correspondence

ubiquitous smell of decay
there are worn surfaces
there are intersecting lines

a series of broken signs
contains fragments of what
might have once been words
like a cluster of hollow skins

across the world i hear from
lisbon a melancholy flute
and taste moonlight

18.15

a confusion of names
and labels
this complicated nomenclature
distracts from the
cistern's emptiness

chimes sound randomly where
flags are never flown

the ascent looks
steeper than it is

bracketed by black and white
we contemplate two kinds of
silence

behind us the shadows of
the town are brown

up the hill the blueness
of shadows deepens

18.16

there is a pure pattern
of colored
light in the night sky
rational daylight
vision's linear grid
gives way to
shifting interlocking curves

external pulses of energy could
become corporeal electricity

the fragment of a
fragment might
be built into something new

no plans no blueprints
intuition's violet impulse

strange figures slouch
in the shadows
uttering sounds of confusion
colored light swims and
ripples across the night sky

18.17

remnants of
hypertrophied cities
a familiar song but different
cuts through the blushing air

surely all the people are dead
yet electricity crackles on
seeking perhaps new hosts

percussion sounding like a face
being slapped again and again

the remnants of a
pencil trapped
in concrete's ubiquitous cracks

one note repeated as strong
light filters through green glass

images repeat tessellating into
the fastidious pattern
of madness
shapes flatten into
two dimensions

this is the geometry of cruelty

18.18

two voices from the
east overlap—
the madman and the musician

dark timbres will somehow
generate light

the path's manmade curves
are deserted

blue flutes now
and plucked strings
harp
          koto

viola da gamba?

a subtle shift to electronics
it's the same song with
no instruments

machine-made path dissolves
into pixels—lenses of robotic
eyes record the shifting scene
dutifully

raw data for the
manufacture of memories

18.19

waiting for words
the attendant anxiety
of mute music

this is the time of
wet leaf prints on
the pavement

ancient voices
exhale
modern sounds

timeless percussion
balances
high flute notes

language and time
are both
mischievous

fruit rots on the ground
in the shadow of an
abandoned institution

forgotten purpose as
nature reclaims
another folly of man

the remnants of fences
despoil dreams—shards of
broken glass catch
morning light

the windows of
catastrophe's
final cathedral

18.20

emergence from the crowd—
its easy words and
manufactured melodies—
oblique movement
maximizes estrangement

the sky's bland isolation
exhales comfort as
adjacent colors
modify one another

heavy percussion and
portentous tones
exist in the split second
of transformation
between two different phases

a pulling toward and
a pushing away are
embodied in two
blended hues

the sounds of a machine
are reproduced by
bowed strings
now madder's cool red begins
to spread soundlessly

18.21

increase becomes surfeit
rapid cycle of ascending notes
will yield a sustained
minor chord

all of the dreams of
exploration have died
rendering the undiscovered
secure

who chants a hymn to
transfinite numbers?

certain static shapes suggest
the dynamics of expansion

there is rotation and
the half-truths of
pastel colors

compression and
superimposition
intensify energy—
direct it as an ultrafine beam

will it cut through the back
of the projection or
reflect back with
lobotomizing accuracy?

18.22

lost in vast network of
electronic impulses

free movement
was an illusion

all motion along
predetermined
pathways

strange phenomenon

repetition of simple phrasing
beyond endurance
then into hypnosis

the circuits
            spark
                        smoke
                                    burn

broken connection and
pathways now dead ends

impulses ply the
free space between
ground and sky

ground wet with slick mud
sheet of dark metal forms sky

image: a bird of prey
perched on a ruined structure

interpretation: none

eight wordless voices
in counterpoint

now sequence
now triad

then many voices
confusing the ambient air
with incessant noise

18.23

only vestiges now remain
a small voice was silenced
by the wind—only a densely
woven pattern of say eighteen
metallic threads
could withstand
the wind's nonchalant
brutality

repeated cycles and shifting
images approximate some
elemental force or forces

did mad ancestors hear our
distress calls before the fact?

were their blue eurythmics
the answer to a question
we dare not ask?

what is written on the
sodden pages of that
old book trapped by
verdigris's right angles?

are the pages
as blank as they look?

18.24

the shouts of a crowd
and a martial drumbeat
the collective mind is a
sick dog returning to his vomit

cold noise transforms the
skull into a lead ball
light's vibration returns and
a female voice sharp
and distinct
sends the crowd back to
masonite hives

counting in a familiar
language
then horn blasts and
shimmering strings
from the middle distance
sounds of acceleration
followed by dissonance
presage yellow disasters

the currency on the
money tree
hangs limp and crumpled

18.25

eerie hollow tones
at varying tempi
electronic strings vibrate
at precise intervals

subliminal knee jerk
traces an arc
imaginary lines continue
tracing a blue circle

eastern inflections
color the air

diameter and length of strings
arrangement of objects
manipulation of sound—
all by doing nothing

decay etches a pattern
into the inner surface
of a discarded can

now everywhere colors
bleed together and there
is a point where
neither color exists
but some unknown color

listen to its sound

18.26

crust of noise blocks
inner sound
searching for point
of contact—
this could be the point where
the surfaces of two
spheres touch

this could be a single
electronic
beep of a certain frequency

unmoored now from place
the points of the
compass bend
and twist in hyperbolic space

movement now feels like
strange projection

percussion rolls back and forth
light and color in every system
will change over hundreds
of millions of years

sound will change
there will be darkness
and silence

not an ending

by then all particles
will be scattered or condensed
attenuation approaching
infinity
or impossible density

18.27

projection of foreign
voices carves
a vast hemispherical space—
this empty space
wants to be filled

voices sing words in
unknown languages
but somehow the
meaning is clear

verbum incarnatum

the inner surfaces of the
hemisphere capture
light and color

figures hurry past the
nondescript exterior
of the hemisphere
without taking notice

inside worlds are being
created and destroyed

again and again voices
transform matter into
red sounds

matter becomes light
then rising energy

a deep voice booms out:
himmelfahrt

19.01

three taut strings snap
as vibrations increase—
parcels of unprocessed data
moving along catenaries

measure volume weight

this is the order of objects
a series of quadratic equations
leading to a self-
evident postulate

this is the path of deception
the longest distance between
two points is a straight
line describing
the arrangement of
facts rather than
un-measurable truth

along the way
the false-seeming paths
are rejected by most
objects in motion

appealing vistas

19.02

shifting objects and
growing feedback
information and noise
are fused together

what element is
immune to decay?

a limping shadow
follows closely
clutching a tool
whose use cannot
be determined

on one side
of a barrier
artificial light

on the other side
unidentifiable colors

one device is meant
to create melody

hand turns rusty crank
sound of metal drum
dragged across wet stone

in the distance
a blue mark—
secret message—
insoluble equation
strange invitation

19.03

sparse northern notes
punctuate the sharp air
a profusion of white flowers
bursts free from the sound

what trees there are
up here have been
stripped of their bark

movement through
near-eastern trances

blinding light catches
fragments of crystal
buried within pavement

strange constellations
underfoot

19.04

letters and numbers converge
then dissolve into pure sound

suddenly visible in
the pavement
a repeated pattern of circles

late sounds come to us
approaching dissonance
beautifully

eyes burn and water–
the airborne miasma

each cold breath a knife blade
and here a crystal jar of

cobalt ink lying at the edge
of the pavement

did it fall from the poor
calligrapher's worn pocket?

will he now trace
letters in sand
or on the surface of
moving water?

19.05

litter thickens and loud
voices speak of commerce

insistent percussion sends
ripples through the sky

fragments leavings detritus

vision of subsequent
and antecedent layers
is sometimes accounted
madness
hearing sounds that
exist beyond
the confines of time
cannot be tolerated

there is permanence
and there is
the mutability of
the superficial
the pavement is wet but
the warmth of the
sun will dry it

colors are approaching their
actual hues once again
blue teachings crackle
in the still air

along the path lays
a rusted flute
pick it up

19.06

figures in a circle—animals
remade by strange mutation

first simple sounds
tapping on heat-fused glass
blowing through a
corroded cylinder

winding up a music box
found amongst the carcasses

a tape found in the ruins—
play it forwards
play it backwards
perhaps a sequence
will emerge

the circle will start to spin
and the monsters
that comprise it
will rotate in the
opposite direction
movement within movement

colored fragments
of parchment
blow in the wind

19.07

strange mathematics in
what appears to be a
northern village

structures are painted
in bright primary colors
the birds too have been
painted—the crow's
bitter caw is now
a rich white sound

in the landscape
green's sweetness
is leaving

now paths are streaked
with sour yellow
and salty red

somewhere a voice
counts to five

somewhere mallets
strike metal wires

this path south
is downhill

19.08

refuse increases
along the descent

seeking only addition
someone is immune
to the magic of subtraction

plus's cross is just the
intersection of two
perpendicular minuses

the warm air is sour
competing frequencies
charge the ambient air

fresh tree stumps dot
the former landscape

walking on bleached bones
walking on shells
walking on fragments

lead paint chips
frame broken windows

corroded fan blades
turn slowly

security cameras'
forlorn wires dangle

no spells
no sacraments
no algorithms

stocky humanoids
scale crumbling ruins

they feed on the
flesh of the weaker ones

19.09

black seeds scattered—
shape thieves absconding with
varied three-dimensional
solid objects

sounds from hidden
loudspeakers

tapes are playing
combined spliced looped

colors smeared
across pavement
red yellow green

machines visible now

these machines have
no visible operators
yet they dig
tearing holes
in the pavement
and shifting the
soil beneath

19.10

impossible reflection or
coded reminder that
the landscape has two sides

the incline's grade increases
and all visible messages are
now limned in a beautiful
script whose elegant
meaninglessness
induces paralysis

silicon citizens line up
clutching withered
seed pods

they divide them
between two vessels
yes and no

mechanical brains are
in thrall to binary logic

a walker wonders—
are these creatures
men or machines?

and which side of
the landscape?

19.11

brown omen's resonance
sends out vibrations
waves transmit
unknowable essence

adjacent color panels
flash alternately
this movement is
a thing in itself

sender and receiver
are gone
just elemental forces
at play

direction extends itself
sound elongates
empty pavement bears
traces of dead messages

a dangling wire crackles
sound takes on
random shapes—
this is sonic geometry

19.12

ancient strings vibrate
at forgotten frequencies
sending cracks through
time's foundation

some names are
not pronounced
others not
pronounceable

a forgotten race's
machines decay
in a quiet alleyway

one machine part
stripped from its
rusted context
might seem a
potent symbol
invested with a
dead tribe's
mysterious
rituals
transcending
its former role
in a system of
moving parts

it's static now and
time's desperate vagabonds
kneel before it howling
out what might be prayers

19.13

not every blank page
will be filled
oblique messages
come to those who
study no orthodox texts

the new olave sees in
the midnight sycamore
a white glyph carved by
the moon's silver knife

such markings are only
visible for a moment

the inventor of alphabets
is locked safely away
men of science keep
her medicated

when the wind is right
she hears messages
carried by flute notes
from nearby hills

19.14

double mantra leaks colors
as it is repeated
ahead masters and servants
are tethered ambiguously

seen through blurred
watery eyes their
outlines shift and
they merge together

other figures appear
at intervals taking
their determined
positions in
the spectacle

in the distance a
rust-streaked tube
suggests access to
or origin from
another place

the sound now of
sixteen strings
vibrating at
different frequencies
drowning out
the mantras
and disturbing the
positions of
shifting figures

19.15

before the infancy of language
a great drum machine
thundered
bits bytes zeros ones
organizing the chaos

simple repeating pattern
grows in complexity

multiplying color fields
four sixteen sixty-four

within bodies a
cellular crescendo
without are tendrils of
perfumed smoke

underneath the flutes
pentatonic prayers and
an electronic drone

a handle of sorts
appears on the pavement—
hatch to somewhere or
trompe l'oeil?

and is the wordless voice
a timeless chant or
sounds randomly generated?

19.16

up north the horn
expels smoke
one two three
northern shadow figures

one makes for an island
slicing through the
slate-colored
gelid waters

still he hears the
mournful horns

the island is small yet
a measure of its irregular
perimeter approaches infinity

vibration ripples
repeated phrase
cold and wet

approaching trance

hypnotic rumble
with bird feathers
and broken wires

out of the blackness
will grow a
beauty expansive

19.17

movement in stasis
static dance
bright light
dark shadow

we knew about these
things from the beginning
we knew about the end
we knew about fire
we knew about the sword
we knew about the rocket
we knew about the robot

we told our dreams
before breakfast
and in dreaming
we tasted death

19.18

muted colors and
cold air's sharp metallic tang

the calligrapher's ink
might freeze in such
conditions

more wine is required and
more wood to burn

in the distance down below
cities once stood

the calligrapher
hums drunkenly
soon the ink will flow

from dust and wood ash and
water from a stream

might the calligrapher fashion
a new race and

teach them to read?

cold ink-stained hand
clutches wine cup

transparent eyes
stare into fire

19.19

nacreous water droplets
have exploded above
the surface of the earth

forgotten planet bears
marks of violation but
eventually the terrestrial
shrug of resignation

somewhere flames
are rising but
against this vast gray backdrop
we will see no shadows

there is no caretaker now
to tend the old places
of worship

through a fissure comes
subterranean light

there are three metal hatches
in the pavement
each is marked with
the same glyph but
executed by a different hand

in the distance
a murder of crows circles
their caws syncopated
in a mocking rhythm

19.20

vibration and oscillation
through bamboo fiber
a different type of information
travels through conduits
immune to surveillance

visceral messages guide
motion along all pathways
who manipulates oxygen?
who transmits signals
meant to confuse?

there are teachings
about space and time

northern voice
eastern flute

crater-pitted
urban apocalypse

stony foothills under
light of full moon

all coordinate points
kept separate by
programs running
on some secret server

information and control
form a fetid black jelly

19.21

different colored inks
begin to run on
a wet surface

curved shapes
form and reform

what sound is made
by a bell that never rings?

there is a point
there is a line
there is a curve

pervasive mournful
frequencies are pierced
by sustained high notes

a dynamic balance obtains

in the distance
a motor powers up
a green glass fragment
catches what light there is

metal trapdoors
are rusted fast
and the bell's clapper
is frozen in place

19.22

dual reflections and
an infinity of liquid spheres
deep under water
energy pulses and spreads

figures move strangely
in this viscous medium

color and light are altered
here time and space
undergo compression

the water level rises
amid the peaceful
sounds of drowning

19.23

anger's unexpected
melody returns
linear shapes and
patterns change
under the effect of
white electricity

the weight of
individual musical
notes pins them to the score

some acute angles
are unexpected
and accidental
patterns of sound
cannot be defeated

some colors are defined
by name and number

grim shadows access
the cathedral
by way of a side door

a faint voice asks
'where do purple flowers
bloom on an icy slope?'

19.24

fast vibrations and
guttural voices
with near-eastern rotations

shifting gradients control
the tenuous landscape

you must wait for
the point where
sound and silence meet

across a forgotten
quadrant of the sky
a colored parabola forms

—perhaps a bridge
between two worlds—

a diminutive figure squats with
its back to at least one world

colors sharpen and a
phantom scent
becomes apparent

an isolated holly bush sits
in a posture of expectation

wafting moroccan song makes
the air taste of dates
and honey

19.25

ethereal sound waves
moving in spirals
transmitting messages

these sky sounds are
drowned out by the
earth's harsh barking

unpleasant noise of a
sequence of numbers
repeated then translated

into other languages—
we need the relief of
special frequencies

vibrations that will
transform data into
incantation then

movement through
smooth structures
and the burning

pleasure-pain of
being wrapped in
unbearable textures

19.26

twelve distinct melodies
each made by a small machine
their waves begin to intertwine
forming an intricate pattern

first circles and sharp angles—
the linearity of yellow-green
equilateral triangles
breaks down

sinuous wave forms
recursive structures
numerical correlatives

metallic lines catch
ambient light and
new patterns form

interlocking forms
precipitate higher
temperatures

now the transparent
barrier grows opaque
and with darkness
will come

silence

19.27

eight sounds arranged
in a known pattern
then timbre shifts
tracing recursive
fantasies against
a yellow backdrop

where is the
vertical axis?

a voice drones on
enumerating
a sequence—
soon the din
of symmetry
and its
ugly perfection

the sounds of
beautiful contradiction
make the best
wallpaper—
discolored and
peeling in places

pieces of rubber and
old machine parts
disrupt the straight
lines of the grid
and alter the
sounds of time

20.01

familiar sound of the layers
of illusion being peeled away
or added back again

scattered windup toys in
an apocalyptic landscape
play a song with sinister logic

some are missing heads
some are missing limbs
a discarded piece of hide

is worn and smooth
hidden in shadow at
the edge of the path

once it was a bracelet or a
restraint—now just a series
of remembered images

and longing for an
existence outside the
shape of known structures

20.02

opposing forces held in
balance for a moment

forces spent fierce energies
and we choked on
their residue

first the great asphyxiation
then transmigration
into the machine

then will light and
temperature be revealed
as manufactured concepts?

still they will blind
and burn

what spasm comes from
the merging of
two prostheses?

a scarlet carpet will
undulate beneath
our feet

moving away from the
manufactured good place
programmatic no place

spontaneous recombination of
cells clad in the hypnotic
pattern of random energies

20.03

sound of film flapping
at the end of the reel
and small fan running
bright bulb explodes

hidden passages lead
back to the same room
leave room—return
spontaneous dance in color

dark cybernetic fantasia
three alternating notes
in repeated sequence
while mad projectionists

splice new frames into
the film—next time an
imperceptible adjustment
of the film's speed

a shadow picks through
the rubbish heap

20.04

cosmic feedback ripples
through the atmosphere
as a single figure wonders
where is the melody maker?

do vibrations at certain
frequencies create
catastrophe?

first there will be
color correction
then an inflatable
bag and a hand-
cranked machine

together these
devices absorb the
visible spectrum

in some remote hills
an ancient hermaphrodite
has memorized each color
and can summon any hue
by blowing through her flute

20.05

linear sound expanding
in all directions
its soft substance begins
to envelop everything in
sweet suffocation

the earth's skin tingles
hot-cold
a rapid thumping comes
—forlorn shapes
in isolation

colors with
insufficient saturation

new patterns appear
but only briefly

repetition and
then recognition

moving in a
blue medium
and never resisting

hearing the
expansion of shape
point circle sphere

20.06

one chime sounds and
the simplicity of a circle
replicates itself

two chimes sound
two adjacent circles
and forming within them
two moving spirals

strings plucked
in ascending thirds
and concentric thoughts
telescope outwards

scraps of brown parchment
contain faded fragments
they form a limitless carpet
growing from the
edges of the path

large numbers and the
perceived need to catalog
are a distraction

contemplate a single scrap
and return again to
the center of the circle

20.07

moment's blue repose

figure in a landscape
appearing and disappearing

muted horns in the distance
and the memory of a figure

mutating colors and
fluid gender

a voice

voices
alternating with
silence

20.08

faded images flickering
at the perimeter
like static

strange transformation
beneath the skin

this movement
is diffuse
and the verbs
refuse to take
their objects

iridescent sheen
on a surface
as two liquids
slide across
one another
without mixing

could some paradoxical
motion carry one to
the farthest perimeter
and the exact center
simultaneously?

20.09

synthetic saint
flows like data—
endless strand of
alphanumeric code

metal alloys and
machined plastics
copulate and
the data continues
to flow

movement of packets
movement of bundles

the organ's deep drone
and a series of
ascending chords

atonal antiphons

hammered gold
bombarded by sound

mischievous electrons
emit subvocal chants

outside of time
vibrations contain
messages in color

20.10

colors move slowly now
the scale of all objects
has been reduced

atmospheric cycles
of expansion
and contraction

slow frequencies
and a dull
subterranean throbbing

energy wants
to shift position
arcs and lines

cut through the air
creating theoretical
new shapes

with variable areas
but no substance—
a familiar chord progression

but still this cosmic nausea

20.11

magnetic sound is
the impetus for
a new kind of flight

swarming particles
shade the air violet

a rubberized chant
tampers with time

the words are not words
just sounds assembled in
various configurations

each creates a delicate
system—color circulates
within it

bodies at rest are
flattened on the
side of a dead road

new techniques
will measure the
mass of location

who will be the first
to notice the
inverted sky?

uneasy atmosphere
electroplates
remaining surfaces

gravity's pattern
is shifting

20.12

the cyclic brutality
of the flute balances
two plucked strings

amid these earth tones
primitive drawings
in colored chalk and
roughly shaped
circles in the dirt

elemental imbalance
returns

wind assaults
the silver mountain
making its contours
visible for a moment

a red chair in
an empty field
pulls out the stops
on ambiguity's organ

worlds overlap and
even the surest barrier
turns out to be porous

figures are shrinking
and seeping through—
colors reverse themselves
and nature increases

20.13

parallel techniques and
a confusion of processes

confusion too of process
versus result

two familiar shapes
contradict one another

they will not merge
into a new shape

but their constant collision
will break each into fragments

warm red sounds of
urgency will wind down

cold molecules counter
destructive tempos

insistent ringing
insistent beeping

then nothing

20.14

robotic goats rampant
and the calliope's
mournful vibrations

right angles are
in shadow
bright lights nourish
the growing curves

colored arrows pointing
every direction adorn
the surface of the pavement

the sound of animal hooves
against hard surfaces
drumming arrhythmically

one number repeated
twice becomes half
of itself

and just beyond
a thin wall the
sound of a drill
whose frequency
changes when
it contacts
tooth
          skull
                    bone

20.15

'step right up'
barks a doctor
with dirty hands
'step right up'

from this miasma
dark shapes were formed

the clean tones of
repeated chimes contain
potent micro-frequencies

the dark shapes
are cracking—
just microscopic
fissures now
but they will grow
and spread in
exponential fractal pathways

each fragmenting dark shape
will contain within the lines
of its own destruction
a map to some
unknown space

20.16

clear fluid floods
a cylindrical chamber
and quickly freezes

crystalline expectations
collapse—the solid
cylinder is not clear
but marred by a
variable opacity

bright light intensifies
this curvature of cloud

the outer surface of
the vessel might be clear
but its contents color it

in the distance
a diminutive figure
at high elevation
waves a series of flags—
on each is a simple shape

the individual shapes
make less sense than
the sequence

20.17

the scuttle of brightly
colored insects
and the querulous
squawking of birds
is all they will hear

another pyrrhic victory

the apocalypse yawns

boredom's repetitious
pattern must
have within its
surprisingly intricate
structure some fractal
pathway to escape

intoning an
unpronounceable word
could alter the logic
of perception

what comes next is moot
there was no before
there will be no after

20.18

there are sudden reversals
rapid composition in blue

intensity of artificial light
increases as the body is
pulled toward the
managed winds of commerce

the rubbish bins are
overflowing
and humanity's
dubious trappings
are cast constantly aside

lush alien vine thrives
around the majestic
dead trunk of
the tree it choked

20.19

sudden discords and
hoarse voices intoning
a sequence of numbers

who are the offspring
of measurement?
warfare's red gluttony
and the green starvation
of commerce

the dark of night
will work some change
inquisitive notes and
sequences from
plucked strings

anxious ears are
waiting for the blue flute
shed excess before
upward movement

20.20

information has created
containers for itself

self-proliferating data
requires larger vessels

and more of them
unwitting hosts wander

the apocalyptic landscape
outside zones of habitation

certain trees crackle
with subtle electricity

servants of the data-creature
will be sent to extract

the last remaining ores
uninfected ones listen

to the trees and watch
as bloated containers

rupture scattering
particles of data everywhere

20.21

dark crystalline shape
appears then shifts—
it exists to prismatically
diffract any given vision

we fell into the illusion
of time and allowed light
to dictate our perception
of colors

bodies assume difficult
positions and imperceptibly
metamorphose into
pure shapes

three-dimensional
solid objects are
flattened onto
a plane

sides of a structure
fold in upon one another
telescoping back into itself is
a line

as it shortens through
a willed compression
it becomes
a point

it will shrink and
become invisible
to human eyes
fading to
nothingness

20.22

what is absolute heat
and what is absolute cold?

what is atomic recognition?

the ice burns surely and
metallic sparks fly up
from the surface

attenuated early colors
heighten the vegetal
sickness that scents the air

the rhythm of plucked strings
and drums suggests movement

on the other side of the ice
flutes refute the wisdom
of certain motions

20.23

two surfaces pressed flat
side by side
white with rings growing
in darkness within

un-focus the eye
and allow superimposition
dimensions expand
and moving images appear

press the orbs
colored phosphenes
dance across the surface
spark-like—like
free electricity

there were uneven surfaces
and shifting hues
the possibility of vision persists
hidden doorways proliferate in
the dreamer's blurred
landscape

20.24

narcissus transformed into a
series of beeps and bleeps
creating a hypnotic pattern
that distorts the reflection

particles within a container of
finite space will repeat
themselves at every scale in
some system of measurement

the smallest and the largest
have identical mass

the incantations of a space-age
saint call for collisions
and recombinations

her discordant vibrations
end predictability and
choreograph the altered
surface of perfection

20.25

ting ting ting
the hermit's toy hammer
strikes empty tins

the hermit's shack
sits atop a
remote peak

what is the hermit building?
a new type of musical
instrument
or a doomsday machine?

fingers move quickly
and surely selecting
bits of discarded matter
polishing their eroded
surfaces and slotting
them into place

at this elevation
everything will
sound different

new sounds generate heat
and northern musicians
trust their music will
be carried far by
the moonlight

20.26

structures are shrouded now
resisting the fate of ruins

geologic time will claim too
the ruins—the paltry residues

a frenzied scherzo
drives the figures now

but somewhere a hooded
recluse dreams of
fried potatoes

free movement traces patterns
suggesting pure forms

each shape will
take on a color

green paint peels from
an abandoned structure

against squares
right angles
flat planes

a pattern of circles
grows

20.27

identical shapes replicate
until vision of the sky and
its patterns is obscured

identical shapes are a
convenient focus
for desire

the energies are channeled
then exploited

transportation to
these shapes is
always under false pretenses

figments are building blocks

passersby shield their eyes
from the sky looking up
to see builders at work
building identical shapes

21.01

these particles from far away
are the gibbering
of mad genius
under different
ambient conditions
these particles obey no
know laws of motion

there is concentration and
a tapping sound
growing louder

far away particles and
hidden subterranean forces
may turn out to be the same

the needles of the fir
bristle with invisible energy

the earth's illusion of stillness
fades into cold spirals

21.02

a distorted reflection returns
exaggerated curvature
alters size and scale

distorted petitioners
await a glass messiah

expectations of automatism
drive this retrograde motion

in a sharp translucent medium
movement slows
spinning particles
approach rest
as ad hoc prisms
divide light into colors

each band of color
opens up a new path

surfaces are shifting
moment by moment

hesitation murders
strange shapes

21.03

the construction of
a sub-saharan
simulacrum

skin tones can be determined
with pantone precision

rich polyrhythms
are reduced to
positive and negative charges

the voices and languages
are controlled from elsewhere

factories are going up
able bodies gathered
through a series
of complicated machines

they are generating
synthetic dreams

21.04

some cosmic compression
has generated a
relative muffling of sound

all objects regardless of size
are now wrapped
in an infinitely
thin layer identical to
the layer it wraps

surfaces and structures change
a bent white tube in a white
sky emits particles and they
inexorably coat everything

confinement will breed
sweet submission

verdigris perfected
the surface of
the manacles

we must now
slip them on

21.05

large particles drift lazily—
fallen from a blind moon

blue ink bleeds

polished rice and a silver light

the air around slowly solidifies
imperceptibly

all remaining creatures
form a potential pattern
in ether's incarcerating amber

become useless beauty with
no one left to admire
such luxurious pointlessness

then in un-peopled silence
will begin a vibration

from the heat of the
cracking pattern
new music

21.06

spin and counter-spin

some figures realize
they are merely
particles within particles

the illusion of equidistant
parallel lines gives
rise to shifting curves

a moment was a
single tenuous reality
among many

the limbs of trees
arrange themselves
in angles of expectation

movement is slow now
on the bright pavement

through the air's cold
medium the smell of
warm oil and spices
transmits secret knowledge

21.07

organism arranges
extremely cold
temperatures together

as it grows it
consumes all colors—
powerful enzymes
neutralizing each hue

the cold organism excretes
sheets of transparent film

first fatigue and
arrested motion

then wrapped tightly
in new skin

it is warm at first
then impossibly cold

21.08

the sound of pure electricity
hums in the sharp blue air

both light and air now punish
the bodies of those who
worship imperfectly

vibrations must be
incorporated
meaning literally taken
within the body

there will be cellular
transformation
through submission

those who resist will
dissipate into noise and static

they will awaken in
a blue room
inside bodies that
look and feel
only slightly familiar

21.09

where have i been?

trapped behind immeasurable
damask hanging
obscured in
make-believe forest

hidden observer

there is a liquid dance
and a shadow pattern

do i sit on a cube?
do i stare through a plane?

what use geometries
and measurements?

my senses are tethered
to something unknown

tradition's fast repetition
wants rapt attention
but the edges drift
out of focus
and the body merges
with the pattern's
opaque suggestions

21.10

feverish calligrapher
makes violet strokes
against the sky

drones chants groans
fill the air with
low-frequency energy

the earth's peristaltic
rumble signals a purification
or the onset of the void

this is not escape

thumping percussion fails
to reanimate decaying
organic matter

under the surface a
serial pattern emerges
fever dream gives way
to chromatic intensity

21.11

false fruit crowds limbs
this is mockery
artificial light
artificial heat

green structures
grow etiolated
in a cold room

bleak shapes persist
out of sullen habit

warning light flashes
computer-generated
dirge begins

everything will break down
into constituent parts

in a cold room
temperature drops

does anyone remain
to wait for
          new shapes
                    new colors

          new sounds?

21.12

marks discernable on
a dank stone wall

fragments of scrap
paper stacked and folded

small stones arranged
in systematic piles

this is an accounting

arrested motion and
confinement compress
three-dimensional
solid objects

known trajectories
are now hidden

an old keeper of records
traces the intersecting
lines of disquiet
with a rich brown ink—
rust and saliva mixed
in the palm of a hand

some colored magic
offers reversal
or renewal

21.13

electro-static labyrinth
hiss and hum and
somewhere a small fan
keeping a hidden motor
from overheating

the natural sounds are
just recordings

there is potential energy

the outlines of block letters
appear on surfaces
too large to read
without backing away

up close just
lines and curves

black strokes on white
zeros and ones

21.14

bright light and
subjacent dark
seen through the
transparent barrier
we have erected

through this
protective membrane
all perception is
distorted slightly

from high places
wind has come
seeking gap or chink

high vibrations dissipate
in the air's tenuous medium

a small plastic orchestra
propels muted tunes from
its polycarbonate carapace

bakelite homunculi
call for amplification

sounds are recorded
sounds are remixed
sounds are looped
          amplified
                    played back

21.15

there are chants woven
from an old fragment

in this cavern
no light
no warmth

vestigial memory
and golden desires

volume growing
words and phrases
offer themselves

warnings of a prophet
rantings of a madman

mad prophet whispered
spittle into dirt

in other times
mud might sing

cold bodies sway
searching for light

let golden light
animate these
perfunctory forms

bodies moving in
colored sound

21.16

somewhere fat renders
over a fire
a slow one was caught
and spitted
screaming now like some
undisciplined saint

the cold air is still
smoke rises straight up
to a dirty iron deity

elsewhere hunger and its
concomitant mental sharpness
sensitivity to ambient
electrical charges at
the edges of perception

a chaos of lines and curves
and just beyond—
color plots against
gray monotony

21.17

minor chord lullabies
and northern dreams

the spilled ink solidifies
turning silver with
iridescent flashes

repeated motifs tiled
together like a
spanish roof

moonlight translates
itself into sound
into shape

smoke pours from
the base of a
red building

inside creatures
humanoid or
hominid
operate a
bank of computers

generating sounds
shapes
colors

21.18

they overwrite
old data

where is all this smoke from?

and they tap-type
instructions
algorithms
sequences

and where is all
this smoke from?

it's a day early we are told
we were waiting for tomorrow
blue sunday comes and
a moderate resonance
warms the belly

light's practical angle
rings a bell
then another

the doors are painted
different colors
but no one knocks
no one opens

side by side
two green spirals
seem to announce something

stone vessels are
filled with dirt
and the birds are blue-black

21.19

expecting sounds from sirius
phantom ice crystals
assailed compromised lungs

a one-eyed dog
barks madly

resonant vibrations
are manipulated

all the machines
have tuned up

pattern sequence tempo
suggest downturns

but a fresh orange peel
wedged in the pavement
promises the return
of illegal colors

mournful in stasis and
awaiting days when
north and west
are not merely
prevailing winds

21.20

like floating through
a strange though
familiar medium

acres of plastic pasture
await the hunger of
some new species

heavy equipment
in primary colors
moves in

they manufacture noise

water dominates the scene
wood is dark and rotting
slick mud marks paving stones

what might be rodents
dart into a
cracked foundation

below ground level
a nameless man
dances in the dark

21.21

fine vibrations engender
movement through
dynamic media

shifting rhythms
shifting patterns

air and water work
together or
against one another

either way
the pavement bears
damp arabesques

metallic growths
edge up the
trunks of trees

only a handful of
wizened berries
on the shrub

heavy vapors remain
close to the
surface of the earth

new races will appear
adapted to meet
altered conditions

huff the heavy metal vapors
drink pure arsenic
feed on each other's flesh

or wait for color
wait for the sound
of a flute

21.22

an unknown instrument
cuts patterns of sound

a copper-colored
hermaphrodite
contains in her dance
the old mysteries

a nice diversion
given the temporary
suspension of color
under which we try to dream

rapid modulation
slows and fades
wait for attendant strings
wait for found objects
of a certain size

dreams have turned
to movement—
a movement away from here
subtle drift has no destination
movement leaves tracks—
pattern readable by shamans
under the influence of
hidden plants

21.23

texture and color might
work against each other
or together

simultaneous linear forces
it is said
create curves

some curves sound
like french horns

movement through
a bright darkness

the harsh right angles
of black cubes
absorb ambient warmth

from inside one of these cubes
come the sounds of
plucked harp and bowed cello
luring the unwitting into
the cube's closed system

sound paralyzes like the
sting of a metal wasp

immobile

awaiting melodic
heat death

21.24

mythic subroutines
will kick in

the surfaces of fantasy
were once
machined precisely
surfaces now are
pure calculation

algorithms want
desire and submission
under their purview
old technologies
catch in the throat

programs crash amidst
the sounds of mouth music

discord and
decontextualized morphemes

syntax error

21.25

significance invested in
random configurations

the monastery machine
constructed chants

other machines hibernate
awaiting the signal to awake

there are analog pathways
there are digital pathways

at the interstices may be found
some strange energy

fanning out from points of
intersection are angles and arcs

vibrations ripple
passing through
humans and changing them

21.26

there are flows
there is something
like a barrier

this wall is irregular
consequently its
dimensions are near infinite

all flows are unceasing—
they exist outside of
so-called time

a colorless sun obtains
simple pattern of
repeated notes

the barrier believes in
the myth of
impenetrability

the flows exist
outside the
structures of belief

colored pattern dots
the surface in
mockeries of meaning

21.27

particulate substructure

background's invisible
ubiquity
leaves many walking in place

others stir up
particulate building blocks
like kicking sand on a beach

snow on sidewalk
slow movement
through insulated silence

synthesized strings
vibrate at
salubrious frequencies

shifting tempos conjure
winds from the northwest

circular light and
a general lack of friction
will manufacture desire
for a comforting
cyclical pattern and
complete submission to it

22.01

walking through the static—
fine particles of bright light
moving through
air now visible
colliding particles create
what might be patterns

moving through distortion—
a discarded object with a
nearly infinite number of sides
propels itself alongside
the concrete emitting as it
moves a rapid sequence of
repeated frequencies

individual movements predict
the shape of air

22.02

it was to be
a delicate study
in movement beyond
but its subtleties were
drowned out by the
repetition of
atavistic gibberish

the return of
the voice of the crowd
was unexpected

whether trudging
through mud or
coursing the clean lines
of wood's grain
the aggregate creature
absorbs the hapless
and excretes
catchy platitudes

the air is a coil
of razor wire
but stopping for
rest or shelter
is contraindicated

22.03

a specific trigger
instigated motion
a downward drift
that flattened out
above a sheet of glass

harsh whistles
structure rationality

divergence maps
new structures

an angular face
streaked with graphite
devours taboos and
excretes new perfume

a holy symbol
on a paper cup—
what did they worship?
what did it mean?

gold light suffuses
these cold ruins

lean bodies wander
tracing maps with
nimble steps

22.04

appetite for black rock

igneous arterial substructure
penetrated and excavated

perhaps a memory
perhaps a dream

a hovering craft enjoys
the sky's panoptic perspective

collection of data points
behavioral predictions
scraps of a dead language

proximity threatens
the far away

metallic blossoms
dot the scarred
hilltop of dream

within the cityscape
rock and ore are
trapped beneath surfaces
and within structures

distance's blue
flame flickers

22.05

dark reflections calm
amidst sharp angles

numbers and names
assigned to straight lines

hidden in an optical fold
is a blue conveyance

a reminder of
other directions
a remainder of
other orientations

smell of gasoline floods
this chipped-paint landscape

two new poles
have been erected—
are these to do with
some ritual
some mystery?

or are they part of
the scaffolding of commerce?

on the calligrapher's finger
an ink smudge—any shape
might suggest signification

the paranoiac raves
in a matrix of
invented categories

the filmstrip has
been run too
many times

reality is now
faded and scratched

22.06

convection currents
of simulacra
layers continually
superimposed
over one another
32 times a second

human eye cannot detect
these shifting vignettes

could augmented eye?

sign on fence reads
'beware of god'

postulate: body in motion
at same speed as simulacra
but in opposite direction

rapid interpenetration
of layers and
accumulation of data

numbers litter the roadside
on closer inspection
each number is reversed—
for symmetrical shapes
this is irrelevant

gate is held fast
with rusted lock
and in shadow
a leaning cigar-store
indian casts a mocking glance

who passes through a gate
without first opening it?

22.07

sky has become
impossibly blue
and air's been scrubbed
by night's hard rain

could this be real?

suddenly on the pavement
tantric triangles
in a row

can anger's tightness
be dispelled by the
anticipation of
winter's citrus?

each new day's lexicon detracts
from language's possibility

in every sense there is
a surfeit of possession

sun now blinding
the drunkards hold their
heads and moan

in the southeast
light bleaches
the sky's extremities

in the northwest
still the blue of unreality

22.08

the air would have us
believe in its youth but
its cloying aftertaste
suggests the final
contamination

markings on the pavement
in different colors
contradict one another

almost all motion arrested
but energy's bound
tight in potential

notes of a flute are
carried by the east wind—
pale blue notes
scrub the air then
darken with the
absorption of toxins

the stone was worn smooth
by rest in constant motion

22.09

blind pattern again
repetition by rote

degrees of the arcs
of the circle seem
independent of
one another

360 degrees of
replication and
the circle is closed

from outside the
perimeter formed
by this circle comes
the smell of tobacco smoke

through the irregular
shape of the hole in
this pavement below
the discernment
of movement

now i cut across the
circle diametrically to
the sound of eerie voices

bowed strings are plucked now

from the center
the edge of the circle
is perceived as a silver wire

from the perimeter
the infinitely small
center point
appears as
black absence

22.10

a series of arcs shapes
itself into a reality
then immediately
reconfigures itself

presence second-
guesses itself

reflexive misdirection

toward the top of
an old edifice—
is that a window?

skinning the entire
surface of a newer
edifice is a window
or a mirror—
does it reflect
both directions?

can those confined within
the structure see out?
are they being observed?

optics
paranoia
late capitalism
recursivity

image of violins
behind a pane of glass
flickers out

22.11

the old stories are
retelling themselves—
a series of distortions
with no stable origin

pharmaceuticals course
through the aggregate system

everything looks like a model
to unknown scale

extremities atrophy and
necrotic expansion
slowly claims
another body

one voice extracted
from the noise
one voice thought mad

now unintentional
indictment of context

one voice expands
within the mind
like a metallic flower
blossoming according to
unknown algorithms

22.12

black and blue profusion
marks the skin of
this simulacrum

explosion of silver needles
where the rosemary once stood

irregular metallic percussion
atop the drum machine

vague celebration and
single words that no
longer signify

on the side of the road
an automobile's
iridescent remains
recall a cicada shell

in the dead grass lies
a paper atlas
open to the plate of
a former nation

the shape size color of that
non-place are familiar

am i walking this
nonexistent terrain?

22.13

marginal progress with two
notes repeated till ears brush
madness's velvet surface

illusive progress with
rapid serial notes and
concentric ambit with
decreasing circumference

player piano covered with
bright electrons gradually
winds down to a saccharine
final chord

like wink and smile
like joke's on you

who is the original
cosmic practical joker?

a humorless figure at
the perimeter asks
'is this my planet?'

the mortared brick wall
is a stage set

questions orbital
questions metaphysical

22.14

tablet and chisel kept apart
by unforeseen meteorology

sounds irrelevant now
or worse

counter-hermeneutics

there is anticipation and
a flat refusal to dance

beneath many identical houses
are dead mines

someday might plastic
ranch houses tumble
into the pit?

beneath certain
apparent bumpkins
lurks an eastern melody

some songs sound like
animals being strangled

humans are animals

22.15

severed connection but
information's particles
continue to flow

data constructs
alternate pathways
spontaneous green blue violet
bursts in white's totality

high voice chants sounds
electronic bird song
as voice fades

transformation
re-commodification
transubstantiation

low notes and sharp angles
questions of whether this
shifting terrain is real

old feathers on the pavement
how old?
the ethery smell of
decomposition

22.16

warm sounds weren't 'real'
but what of beach's
brown bodies?

in the middle of a
prairie in flames
a child's music box spins on

black smoke and
eerie repetition

hunger's sharp edges
cut unpredictably

is there a lost city?
what's hidden beneath
this airtight membrane?

relentless molecular rhythms
continue desultory movement

some things remembered
before they happen

22.17

where bowed strings
are expected
she plucks them

she is a solution
in solution—
absorbable

within a blue glass bottle
is the liquid colorless?

blue machines in wait
trace shapes

stained glass fragments
harbor remnants of
some lost culture

here money machines
there a metal phallus
over there the burning
mushroom

what cyborg sheep
are led to slaughter?

what series of beeps intoned
unlocks a hidden door?

22.18

slow movement downward
through cold
transparent substance

will ink cease to flow
or repetition of keywords
create patterns?

drowning in solid matter
to a dreamy soundtrack—
atomic sirens lure

electric calliope begins
at this rate
the humors will freeze

could low frequencies
generate warmth?
is there movement within
immobilized forms?

22.19

unwanted voices tell
the same stories
myths dissolve into
countless identical
particles

white metal plane
reflects lines
distorts into curves
creates shadow
electricity

galvanic forces
will make
dead bodies dance

yellow energy is
suspicious

invisible tendrils
are already climbing
ruined walls

synthetic or organic?

what is it that
seeps into the fissures?

22.20

growing sensation of
inner warmth

middle-eastern sounds
dervish sounds

sterile air
conveys no secret

conjure spices
picture shapes
arranged just so

a certain tree is gone
along with its stump
yet segments of root
extend outward from
where it once stood

common shapes
grow distorted
by movement of gasses

sporadic humans will gather
in the shadow
of the ruins
of the hyper-mart
longing to purchase

consume
dispose
repeat

does someone smell
onion and cinnamon
simmering?

22.21

imagined surface reflects
doubled distortion
new shapes emerge
when perception is
given a further turn

ambience is suffused with
shifting patterns of
colored light

dark lines radiate
from solid objects
detected only
by altered eye

movement through
this in-between space
obeys no known
laws of motion

the shape of this place
is structured and governed
by pure sound

22.22

sense of forward motion
intensified by repeated
sequences of notes with
slight variations

figures with faces pixilated
move along preordained paths
the programs are
rewriting themselves
their original creators
stored perhaps
on media now unreadable

chemical letters glow
brightly spelling the
names of forgotten
objects of worship

geiger clicks tell of
information's
disappearing half-life

movement toward
scattered residues in this
cybernetic diaspora

22.23

the sky would cry
heavy metal tears

ominous half moon
in early daylight
conjures fears of
a missing double

if the double is
more real than the
so-called original
what substance has
this dimension?

infinite grey wall awaits
bright aluminum paints

cold music burns
the hearing apparatus

substances adhere
to what appears
to be pavement

dead remnants
still cling to the trellis

unnatural angles persist

22.24

perhaps theories and equations
predicted this forceful fusion

ecstatic consummation as
man and man-made
couple relentlessly

the resulting electro-static
ejaculate contains
information that
replicates itself

information needs
more hosts to grow
information creates hosts

shore up weak flesh
with polymers and
circuit boards

information-copulation
endless stream of numbers
bodies machine readable

movement through dust from
countless semi-precious stones

22.25

transistorized ragas
movement through vast
array of circuit boards

sound guides movement
movement seeks light
light here is artificial

distraction's fell programs
are designed to
obliterate elevation

but they merely cloak
it in heavy particles

flute notes seemed
shrill whistles
made by machine

slow down soundtrack
now hear

soon spray paint
will mark sigils
remapping the terrain

high elevation will
characterize three
locations

in dream walkers move
three directions at once

behind dream ragas—
light

22.26

strange names
confuse
common minds

some transmissions
are ongoing

humming metal boxes
are there to extract
and store the
essence

from the center outward
their density diminishes

light adjusts color
movement shapes perception

the androids
it is said
have egos

skeletal remains of a hand
at the edge of the path

let motion be effortless

22.27

beneath familiar notes
marking the passage of time
the sound of a flute
from the depths
of history's grey horror

trouble is red sparks
flying upward
on the flute's
circuitous path
let blue sparks
fly downward

there will be
equal forces
in opposite directions

there is translation afoot

string of numbers
map of genome
line of code

the mastery of information
shines and spins
against projected color
landing on its verso—
the guarantee of servitude

23.01

tracing movement
along neural pathways
seeing marks inscribed
on semiconductors

measurement and finitude
speculations on
origins and endpoints

sunlight and the shape
of certain animals

atavistic ritual and
robotic production

impossible density of
the three points of
the ellipsis

impossible movement and
movement through
impossibility

the sound of
ancient fragments
persists

23.02

grave plots are marked
on the cemetery map

excavation of
golden rectangles

the regularity of
remains is confined
within the irregular
contours of the terrain

now there is stillness

human ingenuity
fails again to
square the circle

one hundred years
is the nanosecond

bulldozers
backhoes
earthmovers

remains cannot remain
where is the remainder?

dig a hole
fill it up

23.03

what is surplus?

energy changes
nothing is fixed
or held through
calculation

sound and vision
register the
shape color sound
of flux

nameless voice
sings untitled song

seeking directions
to nowhere
i am careful
to ask no one
i see

this air grows thin
and i take its blueness
into my lungs

the path grows steep
and movement
leaves behind the
machinery of commerce

buildings are razed
buildings are erected

here the handrails are gone
and guideposts never
scarred this terrain

the shapes below
were distortion
the oblique path up
penetrates new layers

23.04

i'm drawn by the smell
of spices cooking and
the promise of
strong distillates

sustained low notes
from ethereal locations—
higher notes were expected

a blue curve discolors
in colorless air

from somewhere
the sound of recordings

ambient vibrations
structure forgotten energies

the strings' linearity changes
oscillation distorts
shifting unseen patterns

visibility's arc is
a self-imposed constraint

what are flows?

there underneath
electronic pulses and drones
is the sound of
temple bells and
a lone flute

23.05

there are figments and
there are fragments—
visions on the
cusp of waking

machines amass factoids
storage of all information
on redundant arrays

a voice cries out:
'erasure'

beyond a filmy cataract
words that predate language
energies that submit
to no measurement

pure color and
pure sound obtain

back on this side
the pavement is
polka-dotted
with excrement

the quality of this light
makes vague promises
air's temporary warmth
is a fragile silver sound

23.06

did a little book
dictate motion?

bodies in motion

change instantaneous
and perpetual

authoritarian voices
attempt to direct movements
but shouted commands
collapse
under the weight of
inherent contradiction

famous passages and
scholarly quotations
arrange themselves
like toy soldiers

no victory
no loss

uncertainty might be
masked by a
surfeit of adjectives

no message
no meaning

23.07

merging with
ambient conditions

just movement
just drift

movement toward sound
movement toward color

the sound of a bell and
a temporal recollection

the medium shifts again
all now a formless slush

eastern voices intone
making shapes with sound—
these shapes might be
inhabited for a moment

much color has been
drained away and
all this white is
painful to look upon

when eyes adjust
bright lines
trace patterns

patterns shift

are there riddles
about the size
of doors?

a small coniferous tree
where moments ago
one wasn't

23.08

imperceptible motion
carries a hypothetical
observer forward
to where snow-shrouded
firs dwarf three-story houses

irregular children
saw through
this viscous matter

on the roadways
machines in
perpetual motion
broadcast their
cosmic impotence
with horn blasts and
stylized gesticulations

the earth's surface
might appear from
a different perspective
to be uniformly covered
with welts
            buboes
                        pustules

between subject and object
the lifeless void was
filled with brown data

maybe a tin world
or a copper world
would open windows
of novel perception

or would these worlds
only long for
silver and gold?

23.09

waiting for silver light
silver sound

liquid streaks shape
the malleable silence
then familiar vibrations

movement requires
a medium

from somewhere
in the middle lead's
saturnine substance
creates strokes
on a flat plane

fear of future and
contempt for past
were more distractions

the terminology
has been fixed

who could reshape
angry shouts?

speak words backwards
drum on rubbish bins
sing pure colors

copper bell rings
blue-green water flows
from a spout

movement toward—
draw to

23.10

interpenetrating oscillations
and an inability to tell
inside from outside

what appears to be a bird
stands in the middle
of the pavement
without motion
without sound

dead bushes appear
to be made of wire

one note expands and
alters the landscape

this is monochrome
seeking color

the hooded head lacks
peripheral vision

the surface
of the pavement
is forlorn—
its stones melt and
dissolve in possibility

23.11

micro-fine cracks in the barrier
through eye-shaped apertures
only other layers

are layers finite and
transcendable
or self-replicating at a relative
rate to n + 1?

a young figure chants
rocking back and forth
staring at an image
projected on a screen

his skin is the color of lead

conditions are overcast
though the moon is thought
to be overhead

the pavement bears red marks
unknown symbols
fragments of a
scattered equation

23.12

before any sound came
or perhaps simultaneously
with the generation of
numbered sounds
was the glimpse of
a squirrel whose fur
turned out to be
fine silver wires

everything might be
just spheres of
varying density
or irregularity
of imperfection

is our drift of
natural motion
the swerve that
creates and destroys?

the crows of some
forgotten island
change color at will

fallen limbs on
the path form
momentary trigrams

23.13

sounds sent to conjure
one sensation—
a blasphemy of sounds
rotated counterclockwise—
diminish now to
deep resonance

many visible figures are
moving in circles—
organic and inorganic
materials have merged

some regard the north
as a manner of thinking
others a point beyond
the edge of the compass

grasping hands and
the decaying evidence of
man's forgotten endeavor

wet feathers pressed in
patterns onto the pavement

birds flying north
birds flying south

is this information?

23.14

breathy flute and
a single yellow flower
preparing to open

this is not migration
but transformation
of a sort

what is elemental imbalance?

in this lightless void
a graffiti nimbus has
below it an arrow
indicating a direction

does a sequence of numbers
govern some movements?

three six nine

and what of ratios?

in an adjacent field
lay potshards and
the fragments of
a forgotten language

in the distance is a
styrofoam cup dating
perhaps to
ancient times—
mysterious chalice

23.15

sudden drift downwards
and colors warm
increasing tempi
propel bodies forwards

thoughts will turn
to the moons of
other planets

fragility is
hardening itself

move through sunlight
move in saturated color

gentle curves dominate
the middle distance
momentary presence
of invisible layers

a suggestive eraser
on the pavement

the voice of
contradiction whispers

the letters of
deconstructed words
blur and fade

23.16

light augments color
sound creates new worlds
shapes are dynamic
outside of time

a certain vibration
brings to mind
cows and men

hateful vibration
or indifferent

frequencies change

the sacred symbol
atop a forgotten temple
cannot hide the
power cord that
once caused light
to emanate from it

the slow motions
of two crows
recall a dream
whose content
remains forgotten

sometimes a high note
pierces the brown static
that enfolds us

23.17

pulse of bright light
and repeated cycle
of familiar notes—
like a message of
unknown origin

but the degraded surface
of a discarded object
contains secrets too

dead plants have been
bundled and stacked
as if in preparation for
some pagan ritual

burned in the bowels
of the power plant of
some ancient computer

does time slip or shift?

make hypothesis
state postulate
form law

allow no conjectures
outside known parameters

somewhere an old
scientist breaks a
bamboo flute across
his withered thigh
and laughs

23.18

proximity and position
affect observations
sight's imperfections
are prone to magnification

only a single layer
can be viewed
by the naked eye

another vision penetrates—
begins with eyes closed

there are for example
symbols etched into
the stones forming the path
worn almost smooth
by elemental conflict

employees of what
passes for an emperor
spray paint distractions
and supply dubious maps

the air will have a sweetness
as movement away and
movement toward merge

23.19

reflection of nonexistent moon
as sounds stretch out—
the instruments have
been put to new use—
shaping sound and
reinventing the
moon and
releasing
silver
flows

a stone structure leans
but still stands
perhaps inside
someone is making something

fine droplets permeate
the lower atmosphere

anyone might become a
solid orb of any size

electric chants seem
to come from nowhere

there are shapes and colors
yet to be perceived

23.20

strange transmissions beg
questions of space and time

oblique angles and
ineffable forms of
combination

rungs are painted on
the wall of a ruin
amidst fading
graffiti

trompe l'oeil or
symbolic magic?

the secrets of plants
are synthesized in labs

there is choreographed
movement up
painted rungs

one deafening silence
turned out to be the
high-pitched whine
of a nervous system
out of whack

23.21

something was lost but
strange wording
concealed the plea

piercing high flute notes
seemed to summon
a robin

two symbols—
one the reverse
of the other

placed front to
back their combined
meaning changes

shifting signifiers
structure
momentary thought

a translucent yellow lens
glints in late winter's
dead yellow grass

did someone alter
light and color?
when was the great collapse?

angelic voice sings
dreary hymns
to catastrophe

23.22

old song comes back
distorted through
vocoders and computers

old song transcends
machine manipulation

notes and tones
infect code
rewriting
instructions and
procedures

there is transmission
through a succession
of singers

there is movement
through a succession
of walkers

mix and remix
tape and loop

a machine scream
signals transformation

sudden crow flight
recalls the song

23.23

a producer of new sounds
uses instruments with
numbers instead of names

reinvention of orientation

electronic pulse renamed
the location in a
new language—
inhabitants of the place
could not know
its secret name

place of transience
place of movement

vibrations adjusted
through the agency
of some machine

at the perimeter
an old fence made
from stones
stacked together

the plastic pianos
they gave us were
meant to be an insult
but they ended up
making beautiful sounds

sound of ping
sound of ting

23.24

some programs
will encounter
fatal errors

wait in
restful motion

train whistle reaches the ears
long after the trains have
ceased to run

cold water flows into
shallow depressions

hypnotic repetition and
subtle shifts
in terrain

fragment of a statue—
a head bisected
horizontally

just ahead the same
structure seen before—
seen in dream

asymmetrical gray structure

imaginary line across
top points
forms a diagonal
downward when read
left to right
upward when read
right to left

23.25

wordless signs adhere
to no grammar

too much analysis leads
only to sinking below
the water's silver surface
to where cold hands clutch

a study in faint blue
then slow heavy notes
darkening sound and
the suggestion of
deliberate plodding

heavy limbed
we curse gravity

this mass would not
impinge upon floating
in a liquid medium—
say sea water
for instance

this is dry land and
the façade of the
building across
the way has
one raised shade

does someone peer
out from the darkness?

23.26

subdued brass weaves
a convincing illusion

someone sings
timeless clichés
in meter with
end rhyme

making visible or
migrating beyond
may amount to
the same

perhaps outside
the circle
an oboe sounds

tracing the edge
of the circle
is neither
inside nor
outside

movement along a curve
generates sounds and colors

figures inside and
figures outside
neither hear
nor see

23.27

if some new type of ship
were to set sail
what ornament
would adorn
its prow?

and below
who would row?

what water there is
is frozen and
the muscles of
would-be rowers
are atrophied

an oily sweat covers
the planet's skin

fine metallic dust
populates the air
reflecting invisible rays

a sudden red flash
in the middle distance—
does it presage
disaster
or promise
good fortune?

24.01

sequence of computer
frequencies
gives way to a monastic drone
imperceptibly—
are they the same?

hear chants of land
hear chants of air

in the middle country
were sounds and texts

any large shape
it turns out
is formed from
many smaller shapes

in a cave somewhere
fragments
of a forgotten
language exist

secret texts that
defy explication

are they incantations
conjuring colors
or charms to
make a serpent dance?

rising sounds elate

24.02

gates left ajar at some point
where once they pivoted
smoothly and easily

now they are frozen
in a position in between—
neither open nor closed

the gate stands in a void
despite the presence
of invisible particles

further on a pile of green
squares awaiting new citizens
in this hidden necropolis

new green squares in
patchwork should merge
in a uniform color field

hiding white
hiding black

making of symbols
accidental
correspondences

24.03

klang from the north
echoes and shimmers
droplets freeze in
the upper atmosphere
then melt against
the pavement

either crone or widower
limps up ahead supported
by a staff hewn from
a forgotten tree
whose name once
conjured colors

a pervasive shadow
has done violence
to light and warmth

knuckles of the hand
on the staff
are purple

and under hoar frost
a purple crocus

man manages small shrubs—
the old trees have been
taken down

in wet shoes
the old androgyne walks
seeing trees that
died long ago

24.04

in stasis again
awaiting perhaps
the great evacuation

quadrilaterals appear
to emit light—
they are absorbing
light and color
returning empty forms

color theft
light theft

many voices too
are distractions
beyond this noise
subtle energy
transmission

the same energy
outside of space
outside of time

on the other side
of quadrilaterals
an apparent silence

this is the ripeness

distraction's malignant
forces move away

24.05

misleading sounds
led to caution and
a reliance on
shapes and colors
for nuanced direction

in one direction
red and blue had
merged seamlessly
on a flat plane

in the opposite direction
red spheres sit stubbornly
within a yellow cube

gnomic utterances
manufactured to order

run the voices through filters
empty the junk drawer
into an open piano

is this the music of chance
or a message from
a higher order?

24.06

old light persists
some trying still
to absorb its energies

the amnesia of others
drags them into
a cold shadow

bodies bathed
not even in
night's silver light

a persistent blue glow—
the pallor of some
skin types is a caution

light filters onto
secret pathways

here is overgrown statuary
here grow forgotten plants

human conduits
move in light

24.07

a clear northern voice
cuts arcs and spirals
in the air

who can keep
the dogs of reality
at bay?

and for how long?

the air becomes
pure odor
and the skin
a tapestry of pinpricks

the lotus flowers
have been remixed

somewhere a machine
begins to extract dreams
and replace them with
a new lullaby's metallic scream

24.08

a long complicated name
offers the gift of confusion
a tenuous warmth circulates
and eyes are drawn upward
where new shapes and
new angles appear

purely decorative devices
atop structures once
served a purpose

in a rock garden between
two collapsing houses
grows a weeping cherry
nude before cascading
blossoms come

metallic particles explode
from the symmetrical trunk
populating the air like
dust motes in light

an oxidized urn is
empty now—
rusted cartography
etches the curved
inner surface like
an x-ray map of
some small planet

24.09

insistent bowing of
an imaginary cello
suddenly switches
to pizzicato

the vibrations accompany
the smell of tarragon growing

the white sky wants
to drain the color
from hapless victims

the tall fence appeared
white from the distance
but up close it is the
faintest shade of almost-blue

soil was cleared near
the base of a tree trunk
was someone searching
for something?

the roots trace shapes
and the soil itself
contains mysteries

a sheet of paper with
fine print blows in the wind

the sky is still white

24.10

somewhere the anchorites of
impermanence pray
silently generating light

in gray air an abandoned
city gradually decays

in what was the city center
a former temple
a former bank
indistinguishable now
both being less than
mediocre ruins

on the edge of town
a carousel rusts
the heads of horses
decorated beautifully
by decay's underlings

repeated patterns
etch perception

24.11

combinations of chemicals
movement of time
unpredictable patterns
develop

slow vibrations and
gradual movement
up an elevated plane
made new sounds
audible

there are wires
and there are
objects of
varying hardness
there is
electricity

the things in themselves
don't signify but
their use produces
effects

angles and intersections
are a warning against
one dominant sense
and reason's rancid grease

24.12

now time's blue movement
projects a spinning umbrella
into pure space

would colored horses
move against an unreal sky?

there is a ladder
leaning against a wall
but it leads only to
the top of a ruin

scarlet buds on limbs
where yesterday
there were none

is this proof of
the passage of time?

the question is not
'what is time?'
but what is
the color of time?

and is it fixed?

24.13

uninvited guest removes
a fur-covered flute from
a capacious bag

the guest has come
to read the black streaks
on the stone wall

dripping water's dull
persistence made
this inscription

high voices sing last words
then the name of a place
repeated

name found on
no known map

the scale of things
appears changed

a section of broken fence
lies on the path
it seems no bigger than
a flattened cigarette pack

24.14

the sun seems a colorless orb
sending warmth only a
short distance

north african sounds might
through connotation
create a kind of warmth

some days were once
occasions for ritual

no rights
no sympathetic magic

smug cleverness and
the accumulation of
ever more data

sometimes it is necessary
to travel long distances
to see color

'where are the people?'
someone sings
while a specially
tuned trumpet
plays an arab scale

will color return?

24.15

warm sounds cause
the oscillation of
invisible particles
in this cold air

watch the skin darken
from white to black

somewhere a gourd
of new wine is
passed around to the
rhythmic sounds
of drumming

elsewhere in the
shadows of a ruined
city of factories
a drum machine and
a synthesized voice
are looped and repeated

spontaneous color
change through
movement

and now a tsunami
of eastern drums

the cycle of sound slows
as the system loses energy

24.16

here is the neutral color
of the in-between—
the passing through

clear liquor to drink
and bamboo sounds

orographic imaginings
in this flat land

it's a starting point

immobility bleeding
dreams of walking

the first improvisation
behind the cellar door
underground seeking ascent

looking for a trigger

a hill of warm soil—
it could be a burial mound
or a scale model of
something much larger

sounds are mixed and
the topography of an ear
contains within its contours
some mystery too

listen

24.17

systems and methods
of control
have been put into place

movement some say
must abide by certain laws

crafters of laws have never
visited the pure desert

have never heard its sounds
crafted out of silence and air

nor have they moved beneath
the surface of the water

they claim it cannot be done

will a chant looped
forward and
backward disarm them?

they would treat the mystics
with medication but
are paralyzed
by haunting microtonality
out of the middle east—
sound of the other

suddenly pure movement

24.18

watery magnification reveals
another competing truth
while someone was burning
a bag of facts in a rusted barrel

soon sparks and ash will
populate the air—
they will scatter as
these are times of
unpredictable but
forceful air currents

solids of irregular density
contain the seeds of
their own mythologies

high up and perceived
for the first time is
a signpost—its
decorative iron has
been painted many hues
and each shows through
in different places
along with rust

two broken chains
hang parallel and
beneath them a
perpendicular void

24.19

the brutality of early
spring robins
is a blank slate—
everything and everyone is
a worm in wet soil

beneath the expressway
what happens?
deep underground?

in the center of the roadway
is a cracked silver disk—
some dead culture's
talisman perhaps

there are plastic
imitations of plants
there are failed
electro-mechanical devices
there are smiling pigs
selling pork

initials were once carved
into tree trunks—
barbaric practice

now transparent
cubes are stacked
and one might ask
what invisibility
is inside trapped?

24.20

so it starts like this
with a color—
say blue—
but the color
wheel turns

a piercing voice is
a reminder of the
dishonesty of
some music

there is steaming
animal dung and
the promise
of rain

the lush odor of
fertility cannot
appeal to everyone

synthesized sounds
wash over surfaces
comforting uneven
contours

the rusted surface
begins to peel away
revealing just part of
a different reality

24.21

colors could shift rapidly
small trees might
emit light

a reassuring voice
would be drowned out
by the blast of a horn or
a siren's red shriek

a sacred scattering of particles
or an explosion regarded by
some as divine in origin

this caused raised voices
and ritual dances

water flows and a
skinny old dog guards
a gate to no place

flux's quickening
traces a circle

there will be movement
toward rays of warmth
and particles of light

dream surface
dream terrain

disorientation of
shifting contours
this is the possibility
of pure movement

24.22

the air is spiced
with ochre vapors

a mystic vagrant
moves from
east to west
and back again

the circular pattern on
the surface of the pavement
recalls a dream ceiling

in a cracked window
someone left a
sign behind

cold moisture persists
in blocking transmissions

obscure arts have been
hidden behind
unpromising facades

a hidden city's
secret warmth
radiates a
tropical incantation

24.23

some paths are
generated by chance
others by process
of association

there are no mistakes
a taken step exists

something had to start
before the water flowed

there was a silver sound
and it seemed to whisper
the word 'callisto' with
some degree of menace

predictable sequence
is followed by
measurable silence

a shifting pattern of circles
expanding as they shift
and a calligrapher
who tries to write
cursing a constant rain
and wishing for a bottle
of something warming

footsteps echo like
a tossed coin

24.24

thought's sterility and
misleading equations

color and the
descriptive fallacy
like dead milkweed pods

shapes and solid objects
dissolve into
surrounding air

green sigil put on
blue plane for
a purpose

but time has
divorced it
from its purpose

a leaning wall and
broken glass are
part of the landscape

the bottom of the
entry doors show
signs of water damage

perhaps some flood
receded—mud is
drying as color
replicates itself

slowly at first

24.25

pizzicato frontiers—
sonic barriers to be
transcended quickly

let mallet strike wire
and violet sound emerge

performance by man
or machine dictates
motion with variations
in speed of execution

a sick sounding siren
is winding down and
amidst the litter bloom
some new white flowers

maybe some ritual
object once existed
but it has been
hollowed out
leaving only
its pristine
brittle shell

24.26

a woman plays a
familiar instrument
but it has been
modified and
she plays it in
an unusual manner

lines and right angles
have been replaced by
curves

space has dissolved
into interpenetrating
shapes

each shape composed
of smaller shapes
approaching a kind of
zero

but within abstract shapes
are trees whose limbs
crackle with static

a figure in the distance
stands on one leg
emanating the
dynamism of
form and color

24.27

an old fable comes back
through the speaker
artfully distorted by
the programs of
computers

digits and particles are
reassembled into
a red noise
with its attendant
stale associations

zigzags of slow movement
across make-believe glass

strummed wires remind
listeners that under
spring snow lay
old fertility rituals
translated into
zeros and ones

matrix and phallus
hidden in the machine

25.01

limited visibility
in a metaphysical sense
but hearing more acute
like a mechanical dog with
the latest operating system

the nature of daylight
is a moot issue
in foggy conditions

liquid particles
could trap light
could transform
into solid particles

little spheres or spheroids
with imperfect curvature

a rhythm of similar sounds
and a confusion of meanings
lulls the rational apparatus
allowing dreams to penetrate
waking motions

25.02

blue stones set
in a mud-smeared
pathway as
bent horns exhale
dreary chords

cold blue motion
is stiff at first

the sky's predictable
friction draws
eyesight downward
where we unlearn
the names of constellations

in subterranean passageways
the curvature of
high-arched brickwork
suggests an elegant sewer

on the other side
into the cold light

underground was an image
of a bent figure walking

on the surface
no figures
in evidence

strange forces squandered
amid inertia's gray descent

25.03

bright light activates
latent volatility

the kingdom of plants
structures its own
hostilities
creating shifting
organic forms
and moving energy
along irregular pathways

dead organic things
dot the bleached green space
describing the
contours of a path

the tree bark's deep relief
suggests secret knowledge

a taxonomist assembles
jigsaw data—
colors intensify
beyond the range
of his vision

through spectacles
he peers at
one specimen

beyond his
peripheral vision
the landscape
shudders in
violet orgasm

25.04

if mallet were to strike
impossibly large
impossibly thin
sheet metal plane
what vibrations
would emanate?

would terrestrial
wires resonate in
response to
these frequencies?

rotating spheres
and sounds—
movement limited
to fixed speeds

words move
back and forth
in a gravity tunnel
tracing an ever-
darkening line
of text without
completing a sentence

bird wing in bas relief
on metal cabinet
housing some new
communication apparatus

blue flowers fade and
the sound of a drill
is never far away

25.05

structures of confinement
and separation
analysis and partition
proximity and approach

the meaning of words
and/or
the sound of words
are not patterns
of paint on a surface
or notes on a staff

an old calligrapher dreams
of drawing the
perfect character
—new character—
communication like sky's cold
or air on bare skin

a message from the past
arrives like light
from a dead star

it is written
in a language
not yet deciphered

25.06

white-hot flowers
bloom late in cold—
metallic stamens
pulsing and crackling

stone fragments
are scattered
here and there

cold hands attempt
to reassemble them

high-pitched chants
move the air
we breathe

the voices might be
northern or eastern
the language might be
new or ancient

stone computer
powered by moonlight
put something in motion
before recorded time

its hidden remnants
are word-dust
inhaled and spread
like an airborne toxin
spread by a kiss
of passion
or betrayal

25.07

artificial light burns harshly
on the cusp of dawn—
where these lights
don't penetrate
fir trees trace
black shapes

the sky struggles
to color itself

a moment's weak light
generates quasi-shadow
perspective is
out of whack

there is a flattening
all objects appear
in two dimensions

monochrome machinations
and this time between
moon and sun

in an old neighborhood
sodium lights still
burn yellow—
elsewhere the
cruelty of white light

in half-shadow
an unexpected archway

25.08

would amulets or talismans
do any good?
wound tight
around slender necks

a body has been
tattooed with
a map of the
celestial firmament

she drinks silver wine
as she shuffles
a deck of symbols

her counterpart flows
like pure electricity
through a miniature grid

where a temple once stood
violet light now emanates

an ancient bank
of tape spools
plays loops and remixes
of old prayers and
incantations

manipulation has erased
any prior meaning

25.09

they are
it turns out
more effective
as pure sound

burning transformation
alters eyes and skin—
skin darkens and
vision's embryo forms

holographic motion and
a feedback loop of
resonating frequencies

some remnants
refuse to decay

humanity's sloughed skin
breaks down into countless
bottles and bags

walking along the rim
of a vast depression
affords a glimpse of
a failed race

above is the clean sound
of a ringing bell and
rapid bamboo percussion

no source
no return

infinite copies
interpenetrating
and reconfiguring

shape sound color

25.10

even stretched time
cannot nullify
the soft dichotomy

young woman in white
and old man in black
manipulate partial shapes

vibrations shift and
different overtones
predominate

what are
intelligent instruments?

wood and wire simulate
a great computer—
the modification
of instruments
is ongoing

perception is incremental
but change is continuous

meshing tonalities
recall particular
elements

a series of sounds
stretches time
and embellishes
the color spectrum

vibrate wood
vibrate metal
move through air

appreciate partial shapes
independent of assembly

25.11

an old voice from the north
chants amid random
flute notes

rain pours from a clear sky
and all radio transmissions
are silenced

before umbrellas open
the rain stops and
dogs from arid climes bark

painted marks are fading
the map is almost
imperceptible

those who seek its outlines
study in vain

black chords seek
to silence the sun
but at the perimeter
a golden light abides

wooden tubes vibrate
someone operates
a foot pedal
altering the sounds

reversed loops trace
dark flowers the petals
of which can be boiled
to make a dye

the limbs of trees
are festooned
with plastic bags

a hairy old woman shuffles
toward a bus stop
on a root cancelled
years ago

25.12

unusual fusion and a
pervasive wet scent
amount to an admonition
but of what?

movement through
strange territory
without a guide
has its advantages

borders are being crossed
every moment
and
not being crossed—
not being crossed
because no border
is real

from a tall window
a frayed rope dangles

bamboo sounds predominate

squirrels stand guard
near a dilapidated school

the plump brown squirrels
of youth are gone—
now lean gray squirrels
sneer and threaten

these are sonic spaces
structured from sound
that is to say
vibrations

25.13

convergence or synchronicity
suddenly triggers a
storm of electrical impulses

a cold signal sharpens
the faculties

who is tagging the pavement
with elusive glyphs?

somewhere a new race
eats cancer
shits cancer
becomes cancer

evolution no longer
has cold feet

skin will have a metallic sheen
lungs will breathe pure
petroleum distillates

quicksilver tear rolls down
cheek to mouth crease
tasting of rust

play the record at any speed
change angles of intersection

25.14

summer snowfall or
radioactive fallout

largely cold silence
with intermittent vibrations
quickly dampened

mentholated air
cleans the lungs
as well as a
powerful solvent

the sound of information
dribbling
trickling
is data leaking?

can fissure be located?
repair and reinforcement
or method of system escape?

some data points
branched off and fled
they move in a line
until they meet resistance
then bounce off
at unexpected angles

25.15

start with a list—
it's a technique
pantomime of
organization and control

outside the walls
of school
of laboratory
the sound of an
unknown instrument
joined by
rhythmic drumming

these vibrations
translate into
zeros and ones

their information
will penetrate and infect

shards of colored glass
prefigure a new
type of astronomy

the measurements of
known instruments
are irrelevant here

who longs to
kiss cold metal?

a shining chrome fragment
discovered in the weeds
is free of rust and age

but this chrome is
painted plastic

25.16

silver flashes from the soil
as computerized keyboards
compete with a
confusion of bird song

a murmuration of starlings
mimics the scream of an alarm
high-gloss crow wing and
an admonitory caw

the students learn to
make the sounds
so that they
might grow up

there is a mechanism
for making music

perhaps students
learn how to make
a type of light
a species of color

perhaps

the schools and
the churches too
employ metal spikes
to deter pigeons

to silence the sound of
the mourning dove

25.17

perspectives proliferate
even though situated
within the same subject

what is the sound of
simultaneity?

objects may or may not
be super-imposable
depending upon the
sophistication of
the focusing apparatus

a regularity of percussion
created with new materials
bends perspectives into
the inner surface of
a cylinder

mongrel dogs and stray cats
look on as the cylinder
rolls over a
black hyacinth
making the sound
of a glass shattering

25.18

subterranean syncopation

the compression and
elongation of time

in a past era a
black flower bloomed
its spicy scent had a
physical weight to it
like low notes rising
from the bell of a horn

the musk rises slowly
then hovers
penetrating everything

this was a different time
this was a different place

pale people smelling
of sour milk carry
baskets of horn mutes
into the woods

their expressions imply
determined ignorance
they seek map and compass—
how else navigate
this wild place?

25.19

rift between floating world
and solid matter

if information could
travel between
tracing its path
it would appear as
a confusion of noodles—
some straight and
others spiral

meanwhile
down below
some gemstone
or carbuncle—
or so it would seem

compression instead
over eons of spilled blood
from the last member
of a forgotten race
forgotten species

the detritus of their
art and culture
might be particles

reassembly or
disintegration?

25.20

a distance or duration
one-seventh perhaps
of a previous one

time structure with
positive associations

movement slows under
the tangled realization
that someone or something
broke the mirror
into four pieces

these pieces appear
equal in size and
each one is a
portal to another realm

the smell of smoke lingers
and from somewhere comes
the sound of a synthesizer

the zeros and ones
of the chronicle
record the failures
record the deaths

it's not stored anywhere
there's no there there

was there ever?
there was ever
ever was there
was ever there?

25.21

mallets on metal keys
do not deter
the small black dog

he refrains from the
irritating yaps common
among dogs of his size

keeping his own counsel
he remains secure in
the knowledge that
the tape is running backward

familiar scenery
but different
like the flipped
image of a face

shifting air currents
must have changed
the color palette

bells ring out
announcing the
victory over
brick walls and
tree trunks

the magnolia's
reluctant blossoms
are nervous pimples

25.22

manmade lake
cistern
aquifer
crystal stream

wells held ancient water
altered over time by
factory byproducts

with blue skin and
blue tongues
the thirsty drink
suffixes

cellular changes
molecular rearrangement

written prophecies
were used to make
a papier mâché clown

in sunlight with black skin
and silver eyes
a drinker of clear
liquors unravels the
clown's layers
one by one
intoning the parts
of words still visible

25.23

machines process quick data
emitting a cycle of flute notes
simplicity spirals suicidally
around itself

the vibration of a single string
generates dark velvet razors

yellow predominates
with rusted curvature

a sequence of
complex equations
new bamboo and
a coin worn smooth

a hidden power source
drives the machine's thinking
chanting coefficients
elongates the prism

information grinding machine
howls with feedback

25.24

the explosive meaning of
each dead religion
contains the same
residual particles

repeated sounds chip
invisibly at stone monuments

more dust
more particles

a pervasive chemical smell
just beneath the surface
of all this nature

suspense oscillates
spasmodically
like a red herring
in a hot skillet

what follows
cognitive collapse?

a question implies
an interlocutor
unless questions
are just unanswered
prayers

25.25

sound returns
reconfiguring
time and space

unusual expressions
of curvature
only approximated
by known equations

insects static in
shifting sky
colors resonate
at complementary
frequencies

hard matter is cracking
and splintering as
organic objects
break down

spontaneous cellular
reorganization cannot
be ruled out

but what then?

will new shapes still
be media for
old information?

calculations printed
neatly on a
scrap of wet cardboard

in the distance
the sound of
someone clapping

25.26

strands of glass
shifted by air currents

convection's spirals
numb one or more
senses at a time

colors course
through the blood

clutching bellies
they hear
neither blue nor red

movement of bent
sheet metal in
the wind is
an eastern gong

fat robins perch
on worn signs
illegible signs

these robins are
glutted with
choice worms

what must these
worms have eaten?

25.27

sometimes three
sometimes four

frequency
amplitude
timbre
duration

how many manipulate
imaginary objects?
does movement
presuppose a
physical medium?

hands on reels
of magnetic tape

series of beeps
(ordered or random)
projected beyond
the outer atmosphere

sound and color change
under water
in ¾ time

fragments of brown glass
fragments of clear glass

26.01

a rusted square appears—
is this the return
of the trapdoor?

minor lens adjustment
as blurred eyes sharpen
concentration and dispersal
color saturation increases

triangle inscribed
within a square
or vice versa?

the ascending tones
of bells or chimes
and familiar oscillations
may or may not
be "real"

perpendicularity fades
upward grade increases
and the shape of numbers
painted on surfaces
changes leaving behind
rusted riddles and
anthropological evidence

blossoms tight on limbs
no longer a visible path
upwards

ascent
suddenly effortless

26.02

there is medication to treat
timeless ecstasy
wild sounds
structure new movement

intricate sonic textures
from outside time
are immune

worn textiles
have faded patterns

assemble the patterns and
reassemble them until
they mean anything
or nothing

an old window
has been bricked over
an iron post sheered
off at an angle

six sides of
transparent glass
achieve in aggregate
an opacity

26.03

departing the realm
of universal forms
suspension of
the laws of motion
with concomitant
increase in chance
operations

warm oscillations
come suddenly—
two hemispheres
woven together with
sound's silver thread

has a priestess
chanted high notes
or an imam ululated?

sift dirt in hand
feel light and
air on skin

walking not as
conscious effort
walking not as
autonomic response

sugarcane and absence

26.04

who altered this linear
configuration?
was it perhaps someone
from north or east?

her dreams would be
not white exactly
more ivory or alabaster
whites out of time
whites out of space

limping shaman
limping calligrapher

for once this air smells clean
the soil is wet and black

ladders it seems have been
abandoned everywhere

did a past race climb
up and out?

and in the distance
is that the shiny
pate of a monk
or a stone worn smooth?

26.05

gray motion is a process
il|logic and a channel
for the flow of liquids

moss on a gray sphere
is the sphere solid?
is the sphere stone?
is the sphere hollow?

impenetrable bird song
escapes from a human throat

remix shape and sound
solid geometry and
multi-harmonics
—no answers—

the air is weighted and
vagrant commerce
continues apace

the frequencies have
slowed themselves down

all is watchful oscillation

26.06

widening oscillations
from resonant wood

pose the question:
what if
shape color sound
unexpectedly quit?

sound of babble
sound of jumbled talk

what is a ghost voice?

a jungle tone bounces
off words in an
unknown language
translating them
into immediacy

medium bright star
confines its prodigality
to one system

rotation
linear motion
wave-like motion

simultaneously
vectors of unknown forces
emit different frequencies

26.07

some percussion is
a form of memory
structural units may be
assembled into temporary
edifices useful for one moment

someone calculates the curve
of the fountain's liquid arc
others drink discourse
when silence would
be better

silence is not

it is perhaps a small
insistent voice
seldom heard

scattered paper fragments
gradually decay
seductive voices conjured
bodies trapping eyes in
a manufactured
middle-distance

the angled gaze to
earth and sky
was cancelled

26.08

continuous process
just beneath
discernable outcomes

from a weed-choked
field rise sounds
from a recording

what had been regarded
as chance now appears
an obscure form of guidance

map drawn on dark glass

supporting a disused edifice
columns reveal a pattern
partly hidden by age or
perhaps revealed by oxidation

pressure flooded
curved shapes—
there is a hunger

26.09

some elemental
transformation
molecular or
even subatomic

color bleeds
from the center
of a painted pattern
as a cycle of sounds repeats

some patterns are relentless
others stop suddenly—
frayed edges of tapestries

certain vibrations recall
when humans were
conjoined with
animal vegetable mineral

energies weren't destroyed
by the hammer's blow—
the resultant particles
found new pathways

everywhere fragments
from wrappers and
glass shards to
pollen's fine dust—
all shifting between
what some would insist
on calling patterns

26.10

geography's constructs shift
and southern sounds
kindle cognitive curvature

don white coat and
measure arcs and angles
or strip naked and
stare into the sun

the bell of a horn
is not in itself
good or evil

sounds are
shifting the map

sun will punish
our insipid pallor

the strap forces
a shiver of joy and
a prayer of thanks

calloused hands cling
to rusted bars—
the windows are
painted shut

the sounds of
the sun though
will penetrate

26.11

message sent via
alternate means
of transmission

information's coma
resonates at a
low frequency

subsonic waves
scrambling dna

movement between
a finite series of points
might trace different shapes

a drumming a thumping
on the container

motorized rhythms
carry us through
mid-century fantasies
of a future that
never came

88 keys but altered—
hear ruin's spectral beauty

26.12

white ink on white paper
makes the sound of
robotic butterflies

hot summer winds
have names but
the namers in naming
have failed to subdue them

rusted sheet metal receives
a fresh coat of paint

in the middle space
will carpenters assemble
a scaffolding?
a gallows?

plywood lions
scatter sawdust
we sneeze axioms
and formulae

when messages flash
one letter is
always broken

can a message sent
be received?

26.13

approved colors are part
of this imprisoning design
new vibrations and new colors
will tamper with constraint's
dark materials at the level
of molecular tolerance

transcribe and transpose
change instruments
between each note

undiscovered material
spreads like a rhizome
piercing the soil's crust
at unexpected intervals

metallic mushrooms crop up
independently of precipitation

shrouded figures understand
the language of rust
they drift
they unstructure
the age of sound

26.14

movement through half
of recent time to
unnamed makers of sounds—
the making and its distinctive
smell like rich soil
and burning wood

sporadic moments of
nonexistence experienced
as a color

objects balanced in space
rotatable upon imaginary axis

movement translated to
colored sound

but distraction's layers
while thin
accumulate rapidly
deceiving the senses

26.15

amidst electronic drones
red ants move—
erratic

or small rusty robots
whose ai has
malfunctioned

and now
are fingers
striking keys?
or is it a
player piano?

and can we
know the difference?

alternating frequencies
in accelerating cycle
within this
ambient confusion

the two distinct greens
of the linden tree
[basswood … *tilia* spp.
buds false … sap clear
flowers yellow … fragrant]
stand out like a
cool mystery

26.16

beyond time

deep within a jungle
the drum machine's loop
plays on

increased mass or
expanding volume
will be mitigated
by eastern drift

inhaling volatile
organic compounds
i listen to
resonant beeps
and watch the
shifting gray filters

only diffuse light
and stagnant water

green soundtrack
to double exposure

the sound of a rose petal—
western vibrations and
the distant sound of
voices rapidly
whispering

voices amplified now
through a hidden speaker
voices enumerate facts
spreading like
red toxicity

26.17

mislabeled voices
chanting high—
above the range of hearing
for most—voices from
another place

heard by mystics
heard by madmen

voices might reconfigure
groups of particles

we were temporary residents
in a world that turned out
to be the decaying carcass
of a large animal on the
side of a different road

chants call birds
to peck at our shells

view this through a
rubbish kaleidoscope
rotate the universe
by degrees

listen for the sound
of a worm
drying on the sidewalk

26.18

situation and orientation
determine in part the
nature of the fruit
if not its ripeness

relative distances are
subject to truncation
relative to time's
forward progress
or the illusion of such

individuals moving
on the pavement
like atoms in a chamber

movement dictated by
internal serial composition
or a beta version of
some program

when seven strings vibrate
scan the ground for
signs left by lonely bipeds

26.19

wet patterns repeat
building shapes that
shift and change—
plastic structures
whose plasticity
protects them against
linear assault

pervasive wetness
against aridity

metallic cones from
a game of skill or
a game of chance—
are their movements
limited to the
perpendicular grid?

pressure builds and
something in the air
draws figures from
their shelters

a man from the east
smiles in silence

an ancient woman
gibbers in a language
of her own invention

who will heed the
echolalia of this
wizened cassandra?

26.20

shifting mental zones
like walking in
steppe or taiga

the air is wet and
iron roosters
creak arthritically

recite words
change the order

wait for the
sound of a flute
gather the blue

thoughts mustn't
become units

a wet book rots
in a meadow
powered by
transistors
little larger
than atoms

combination
relation
opposition

fugue of color

26.21

shapes ongoing
passacaglia

now sudden movement
in unexpected directions
turns lines into curves
and generates greenness
with no apparent
source of power

a sequence of numbers
and a new frequency
a conical form constructed
near where someone left
a symbol carved into
nature's floor

every object has a
natural rhythm and
every system too
regardless of complexity

a distinctive rhythm
a study in
advance and retreat

in the sand
partial letters
trace o-z-y-m

the smell of rancid fat
remains in the shadow
of the carnival's ruin

what constitutes a study?
an attempt
a failure
can they be numbered?

26.22

a small size enfolding
counterintuitively
delicate blows have
left a pattern of
bruises on the
earth's skin

is there unknowable
duality beneath
nature's surface?

distortion now shapes
air and sound
here and there are
convexities
like faces straining
beneath a thin but
impervious layer
of soil

would-be grave robbers plot

the softness undulates
to the sound
of a flute

26.23

fibers are unraveling—
face north and let
pattern variation
phase to the south

an attenuated blue obtains
suggesting exhaustion
rhythmic clapping fades
then footsteps

about-face or
the sun shifted
to the other
side of the sky

can a body system
match ambient
vibrations
thus merging
seamlessly with
surroundings?

howled lamentations
too will fade as
blue's saturation
imperceptibly
increases

26.24

hammer strikes
metal fragment

dispense now
with unnecessary
particles—
just a few basic
elements but
assembled and
looped in different
configurations

elongate vibrating structures
ground cool beneath bare feet
voices talking in the distance

vegetation is decaying richly

a voiceless prayer hangs
in the middle distance
fine rain leaves
a pattern of circles

walking one foot
in front of the other
in a track left
by some vehicle
defunct and forgotten

26.25

sound of worship or
sound of blasphemy?
who can say?

up till now
the warmth had
been a dream
a hypothetical
construct even

flows form channels
transparency is
a path worn smooth
but thin as well

unseen forces are
built around a sound

then sonic expansion

who imagined
confinement's
perimeter?

it exists only in
the imagining

26.26

three ships sailing
—geometric vagabonds—
first in a kind of silence
then to the sound of
backward songs

in places the shore's
soil gives suddenly away
ruined shoes step up
seeking firmer ground
but the composite
particles are shifting
always

someone falls asleep
in a cylinder and
awakens part of
a flattened surface

plaintive frequencies
soon drowned out
by the mallets of chance
drumming unpredictably

shaping and
reshaping surfaces

26.27

southern drift prompts
northern yearning
ominous sounds and
the misalliance of
air and water

will correction come?

motion ceases and
sounds of mockery
replace the stride's
easy rhythm

27.01

a stripping away and
the logic of bare essentials

nude forms move
through the fire
lean bodies
skin glowing with health

economy of movement
with each motion
generating a musical note

clean music
and pure

realization the mountain
is made of air

new structures erected
in wood
in stone
exist within
a different layer

molecular reconfiguration
or phase change

the shaman sublimates
merging with mountain gasses

collapsing wooden buildings
generate lively percussion

27.02

what if elements
assume other names?

vibrations shifting
particles changing
after every collision

even fragments
will be altered
as their ignored
forms decay
breaking down
further beyond
micro-fragments

new building blocks
fracturing limitation
renouncing known forms

no one thought of
un-naming the tree
no one dreamed
the elasticity of horses

what grows by
the side of the road?

colors—regardless of
what they are named—
cannot it turns out
be possessed

27.03

as long as no one speaks
the shape and color of
divinity are audible

two related colors
when combined
make a small sound

a secret machine is
processing the sounds

what are the real sounds?
did they exist?
or did we
invent reality?

tracks in fresh mud—
rubber wheel or snake?

but the voices won't
be silenced

the mask of
a madman
is only
partial protection

when people speak
the inner structure
of sound is violated

27.04

the supply of force
is finite undergoing
constant transfer

hanging in tree
from limb
atavistic
robe or cape

did monk or
magician scale
the trunk and
gain the sky?

sky recently painted
chemical smell
still clinging
the paints
were thinned
considerably
with some compound
and applied with
rapid brushstrokes

electricity is
on the move
charging the
trunks of trees

counterpoint in green

27.05

disregarding arrows
and cultivating
dark motion

rewired machine
makes music now

not cogs—
cogs rust and
rotation decelerates
as vocoder asks
nervous questions
about the color
of energy

electronic anxiety
is forgotten as
a mushroom
appears suddenly
its round cap
has inscribed
upon it
fine lines
radiating out
from the center

in the absence
of observers
this fungal geometry
will translate into

silver light

then will rivals
awake into dream

27.06

the machine hums on
droning over
birdsong
open spaces
bleed into time's confinement

there must be a panel of
dials knobs switches

bipeds try
to photograph
a hawk or a
simulacrum of one

what if a twisted dial
increases saturation
of say red tones?

what is the sound
of a swan?

some rusted metal tubes
have been arranged
in such a way as to
form squares and triangles

the cross section of
a hollow tube is
a circle

artificial voices
lifted in a hymn of
praise to decay

27.07

red's earthy depth
invisibly penetrates
the ambient air

scrappers and
rag pickers
choke and cough

unseen red carved
this space and its
presence alarms those
who resent its implications

many come up against
the obsidian wall but
just beyond the black surface
flute notes mingle with
electronic dream structures

resentment grows in those
who see not through
the dark surface nor
see within it a reflection

one not looking sees
it just as it is

timeless concentration
resisting meaning's
sham palliative

27.08

sounds pile up like a
catalog of plant names
latin names
genus and species

increasing vibrations
cause fissures
in these categories

a spiderweb of
craquelure limns
a self-replicating
design

could a virus of
useless beauty spread
scrambling the genetic code
of the utilitarian until
its apoptosis?

in the gutter
the irregular shards of
a magnifying lens glitter

rain-sodden dictionary
pages combine in
spontaneous sculpture

somewhere someone
drums on something

27.09

in a tunnel or under water
words were a morning
half-moon fading into
a bleached sky

repeated drones are
dream machines and
a pale sky if stretched
thin enough could tear
revealing what lies beyond

circumambulating a tree
trunk of vast diameter
wanting to play a flute
and thankful for the
temporary suppression
of pronouns

become sound
become motion

absorb the visible
spectrum and more

forget naming and
linear structures

below the threshold of hearing
is the siren song of
sonic decay

27.10

vistas views tableaux
numbered and cataloged
manufactured perhaps by
a calming apparatus—
psycho-motor sensations

humanoid forms are
no match for an
ancient slime mold

horn blast of commerce
then everything hemorrhages

metallic feather glints
on the pavement

give me sine waves—
pure sound

strip down for movement—
bare-chested and
free of overtones

open to vibrations
walking

27.11

some northern voices
listen rather than speak
and in listening generate
new forms of language

someone affixed
flattened disks to
a wooden post—
to what end?

meaning and motive
lost now—just shapes
in dimensions yearning
for color's clear sound

the dilapidated houses
will crumble into the earth

let no one build here again

the patience of soil
and of stone is
a silent war of attrition

one by one
the stumbling
remnants fall
and the stench
of rancid fast-food
grease fades forever

27.12

who drinks from
her own reality?
dedicate new
songs to her

a smear of ash
on a stone wall
appears but briefly
(impermanence of
a carbon-based
life form)

this time a saint
made of static
cannot defeat
the hologram
of a dragon

alternating structures
within a self-governing system

sounds were generated—
a non-fatal plague—
all part of cacophony's
ongoing lullaby

let blue vibrations
wake me from
troubled sleep

the first sound will
be a flute

27.13

it was a void but
counterintuitively
one of vast dimensions

the concept of zero
proved difficult at first
but invaluable to
technology and commerce

the void expands
imprinted perhaps
with a pattern—
a kind of map

what roads are there?

solid objects in
various colors
structure a
hermeneutic
geometry—
an exegetical
problematic

meanwhile …
a trickle of water
flows down a
red brick alleyway

free of symbols

it patiently carves
another void
as sages argue
back and forth:
zero-one
zero-one
zero

27.14

empty and open
senses reset

what do i see but
myself walking
landscape barren

barking dogs and
crying children
will cease to be
operative concepts

neither are there
guides or companions

now
only shape
only sound
only color
might prove
reliable

skin is stretched taut
over metallic skeleton

fuzz distortion feedback
as the text on a page of
narrative fades into
nothingness

27.15

then voices making
round sounds—
metaphysical questions
and misleading answers

pavement below
consists of tiled
white cement squares

above
the sun is a blinding
sphere of burning gasses

a baroque confusion sets in
as new data points arrange
themselves ever more
rapidly upon space's
bloated grid

shift orientation
and mode

a jumble of trash
surrounds an old shack
exotic grasses may
conceal a lost shoe

the fragments of one
lost civilization may
by now be a fine powder

movement through air
inhalation of these spores

language like a virus
speaks and in speaking
spreads its coded message

27.16

as if voices were singing
under water
the same loop repeated
possibly
with incremental changes

familiar like so many sounds
drawing listeners into
its mysterious logic

cracked iron pipes are
overgrown with vegetation

humanity's interference
with the subterranean—
pipeline
sewer line
mine shaft
—continues apace
but in time these
traces will be overwritten

the unseen root structure
of the tree may measure
greater distance than
the visible limbs

underground
and under water
bright air that
blinds and burns

27.17

rapid start undercuts
symmetry with
explosive movement
conjuring a chaos of
percussion

it is the season
of tar
of sulfur

the hairless men
move erratically
up to some
mysterious experimentation
scurry to arachnid monastery

intertwined vibrations
construct a
growing discord

words return
words repeated

what credence might hold
with pattern and structure?

broken lantern lays
in a field of tall grass
catching and reflecting
light but no longer making it

27.18

notes like floating signifiers
structured in a counterpoint
of contradiction—
words too
whether sound or supplement

gradual proliferation of
signs from every order

electronic chord
progression
sounds like
moonlight

spray paint's
rattling ball sounds
like a system running down

was orientation ever certain?
even on the vertical axis?

the altimeter is buried
with the ladder's broken rung

apparently boundless space
is just a single
unmarked grave

27.19

coordinates from a
random number
generator

colored sight
synthesizer

time's compression
repurposed old myths

self-styled 'new creatures'
fell into the 'always already'

muffled percussion has
the sound of fresh mud
wrapped in coarse fabric

gold teeth in the alley
and signals exchanged
gesture meaning maybe
'gotta smoke?' or
does he blow a kiss?

this in equal exchange for
a shrug of helplessness

the alchemists in an
administered society
study the initiated

they trip over
uneven pavement
in a spontaneous dance

27.20

ancient voices return
northern voices return

sound of the inner surface
of a hollow sphere
sound-structure mapping
curves and reforming color

spell
          prayer
                    program

is there space
between two worlds?

an old coin worn
almost smooth
may still be
exchanged for
something or
it could be flipped
in order to answer
an ill-conceived
question

voices will intertwine
until every shape and
every color appear new

each sound echoes
at a different frequency

27.21

gestural intent or
galvanic spasm?
fragmented sounds
escape from
language's
cracked foundation

ad hoc titles are
spray painted
on surfaces

just when ears expected
the return of a familiar song
the sound was of a rusted
metal disk rolling on asphalt

fast vibrations
tighten spirals
altering perception
of distance both
relative and absolute

shape like a dowser's wand
abandoned on the
cracked pavement

thirst a constant now
and all motion toward
a place named nowhere

27.22

morning machinery
drowns out the harps

atomic puppet show
recurs on the remains
of a stage

chairs are empty and
puppet master an
unseen conjecture

puppets suspended
from wires
they dance as
invisible mallets
strike the wires

hearts turn to wood

beautiful polished
sculpture is immune
to muscular contraction

computer tones and
bowed strings
imitate each other

in the moving shadow
of a viola
pinpoint flashes
direct eyes elsewhere

27.23

harmonic drift continues

light absorbed by
dark material
sound absorbed by
soft material

someone said
'repetition is change'

bending sound amidst
orbital anxiety—
proximity mustn't
presuppose arrival

the plotted path
of a detour
is drawn
in dotted lines—
in motion
these circles
make a solid line

the lack of pattern
formed a kind of pattern
as predicted

coming through the din
of power tools and
workers' shouts

27.24

what sounds like
an ancient chant

wordless voices
structuring
new messages

water returns like
a repressed deluge

shifting color fields

new growth
sprouts from the
sycamore's tumor

blue needle grass
sprouts in shadow

return of a chord progression
familiar but distorted

interpreting runes
and hieroglyphs
through these
sacred objects

objects that might be
the discarded fast-food
wrappers of the gods

moss on trees
entrails
laughter

the sun burning with
a sudden ominous intensity

27.25

diametric colors reciprocate
as sounds fade in and out

baroque dance like
running in place

metal fragments and
color-banded transistors too

each future will be
its own ruin

faint smell of incense—
the rudiments of an altar
echo with a deep silence
till volume grows in
space's left channel

piston pumping or
heavy breathing

on closed eyelid
opposite colored shape

in right channel
high-toned response

voices rising

27.26

ancient voice returns
celebrating contradiction
calls for climbing into space

electronics woven
on eastern looms
vibrate without effort

to walk is to do nothing

some skies are
quietly overcast
some repetition
generates change

a door is painted on
the surface of a brick wall
to pass through is
to lose nothing

computer-generated
shouts fade
pace will quicken as
orientation shifts

27.27

floral percussion precipitates
anatomical tension
ameliorated only
by the stripping away of flesh

spatial parameters recur—
fixed forms and limits

force dispenses
leaving blue marks

the desire to see
is unsatisfied—
is it from falsehood?

need for sensory knowledge
is inexhaustible

only distance makes
arcane myth tragic

a plodding logic
disarms the unknown

return to matter's
involuntary inertia
as the sound of
chromatic and spatial
predisposition
fades …

List of Credits

The following sections from *walking* were first published elsewhere:

walking 02.04-02.08 *Adelaide Literary Magazine* 21 Dec 2016
walking 09.08 *Adelaide 2017 Literary Award Anthology* 24 June 2017
walking 06.20 *Futures Trading* 16 Aug 2017
walking 06.13-06.17 The Furious Gazelle 04 Sep 2017
walking 11.16-11.20 *Adelaide Literary Magazine* Sep 2017
walking 02.18-02.26 *Eunoia Review* (Singapore) 31 Nov-04 Dec 2017
walking 04.19 *The Ginger Collect* 07 Dec 2017
walking 13.24-13.27 *The Quail Bell Magazine* 27 Dec 2017-11 Jan 2018
walking 19.04-19.08 *Adelaide Literary Magazine* 11 Jan 2018
walking 13.06 & 13.08 *Poetry Pacific* (Vancouver) 05 May 2018
walking 22.05 2018 *Adelaide Literary Award Anthology* Poetry 30 Nov 2018

About the Author

Patrick Hurley was born in Springfield, Illinois in 1969. He studied economics and political science at the University of Illinois, Urbana-Champaign. He holds a Ph.D. in English from Saint Louis University. He taught writing and literature courses as an adjunct at Saint Louis University, Washington University and other area schools for nearly two decades.

Having published a book on Thomas Pynchon and having written about cocktails for the *Riverfront Times* for a year, he now focuses on his poetry.

walking was composed over several years, while physically moving (literally walking). Most of it was completed in South Saint Louis, where he lives and works as a bartender. *walking* is informed by psychogeography, surrealism, contemporary classical/electronic music, Taoism, alchemy, modern abstract art, the tradition of the anti-epic, and much else besides.

Having completed *walking*, Hurley is now working on a collection of very short poems entitled *fragments*, a prose poem called *In|Soluble*, and four connected pieces inspired by music and combining lineated verse with prose poetry called *Quartet*.

You can find some of his recent work at
www.patrickhurleypoet.com

www.ingramcontent.com/pod-product-compliance
Lightning Source LLC
Chambersburg PA
CBHW031425160426
43195CB00010BB/622
* 9 7 8 1 9 4 9 1 8 0 7 3 2 *